MW00648306

J. Josh Smith

THE TITUS TEN

Bible Study

FOUNDATIONS *for* **GODLY MANHOOD**

Lifeway Press® • Brentwood, Tennessee

EDITORIAL TEAM

J. Josh Smith
Writer

Jon Rodda
Art Director

Reid Patton
Senior Editor

Tyler Quillet
Managing Editor

Brett McIntosh
Associate Editor

Joel Polk
Publisher, Small Group Publishing

Stephanie Cross
Associate Editor

John Paul Basham
Director, Adult Ministry Publishing

Published by Lifeway Press® • © 2024 J. Josh Smith

No part of this work may be reproduced or transmitted in any form or by any means, electronic or mechanical, including photocopying and recording, or by any information storage or retrieval system, except as may be expressly permitted in writing by the publisher.

ISBN 978-1-4300-9279-7 • Item 005847235

Dewey decimal classification: 248.842
Subject headings: BIBLE. N.T. TITUS--STUDY AND TEACHING \ MEN \ CHRISTIAN LIFE

Scripture quotations are from the ESV® Bible (The Holy Bible, English Standard Version®), copyright © 2001 by Crossway, a publishing ministry of Good News Publishers. Used by permission. All rights reserved. Scripture quotations marked CSB have been taken from the Christian Standard Bible®, Copyright © 2017 by Holman Bible Publishers. Used by permission. Christian Standard Bible® and CSB® are federally registered trademarks of Holman Bible Publishers.

To order additional copies of this resource, write to Lifeway Resources Customer Service; 200 Powell Place, Suite 100; Brentwood, TN 37027-7707; fax 615-251-5933; call toll free 800-458-2772; order online at lifeway.com; email orderentry@lifeway.com.

Printed in the United States of America

Adult Ministry Publishing • Lifeway Resources
200 Powell Place, Suite 100 • Brentwood, TN 37027-7707

Contents

About the Author

J. JOSH SMITH is the pastor of Prince Avenue Baptist Church in Athens, Georgia. He is the author of *Preaching for a Verdict*, *The Titus Ten*, and co-author of *Psalm 1–50* in the Christ-Centered Exposition series. He and his wife, Andrea, have four daughters and one son.

How to Use This Study

This Bible study provides a guided process for individuals and small groups to embrace ten foundations for godly manhood. Ten weeks of study give a biblical framework and practical guidance for what it means to be a man. Through the study, we will see the kind of men that God has made us to be.

GROUP STUDY

Regardless of what day of the week your group meets, each session of content begins with the group session. Each group session uses the following format to facilitate simple yet meaningful interaction among group members and with God's Word.

START

The group session will begin with a few questions designed to help you introduce the session's topic of study and encourage everyone to engage with the study.

WATCH

This page helps you follow the video teaching session and provides space to take notes. Codes to access the teaching videos are included with your purchase of this book and can be found on the insert located at the back of this book.

DISCUSS

This section is the main component of the group session. The questions provided are designed to facilitate the group study of the session's topic. The goal is to better understand God's heart for men and helps you apply the biblical teaching to your life.

PERSONAL STUDY

The group and personal studies are complimentary. Five days of personal study are provided after each group session to help individual men think biblically about the session's topic. With biblical teaching and introspective questions, these lessons challenge individuals to grow in their understanding of God's Word and to respond in faith and obedience.

LEADER GUIDE

In the back of this resource, you will find a guide for potential ways to use this resource. Josh has taught this study over many years in several formats. See the leader guide for proven ways to lead this study and decide what works best for the group you are leading.

The Titus Ten

Dominion

Group Study

START

Welcome to week 1 of The Titus Ten.
Use this page to get the conversation going.

Welcome to the first week of *The Titus Ten*. Each week we are going to discuss one foundational aspect of what it means to be a godly man.

What does it mean to be a man?

What is your definition based on?

To understand the kind of man God *wants* you to be, you must understand the kind of man God *created* you to be. That means the journey to manhood must begin with the creation of man. Almost everything you need to know about manhood has been clearly articulated in the first two chapters of the Bible.

In Genesis 2 we get a picture of God's original intentions for manhood. But we must look fast—the picture does not last long. Starting in Genesis 3, the rest of the Bible shows how God's original intentions have been distorted. And because we see the distortions on every other page of the Bible, and in every man around us, we tend to focus more on the distortions than the intentions. But our goal is not to tear men down; it is to build them up. We are trying to lay a foundation on which to become godly men, and we must begin with God's original intentions. That starts with dominion.

WATCH

Use this page to take notes as you watch video session 1.

To access the teaching sessions,
use the instructions in the back
of your Bible study book.

DISCUSS

Use this page to facilitate the group discussion.

Read Genesis 2:1-17 together.

What do you see about manhood from those verses?

Mankind was created to have a relationship with God, to live under God's authority, and to have authority over everything God created (Psalm 8). Adam found his true identity in his relationship with God, and he was to fulfill his God-given assignment by ruling over God's new creation on God's behalf. As he did, God's glory would spread to the ends of the earth (Genesis 2:10–17; Habakkuk 2:14).

The responsibility God gave to Adam and Eve was clear: "Be fruitful and multiply and fill the earth and subdue it, and have dominion over the fish of the sea and the birds of the heavens and over every living thing that moves on the earth" (Genesis 1:28).

Dominion is not domineering. How do the two differ?

When God called Adam to work and care for the earth, what would have been some of his responsibilities?

How would the responsibilities God gave to Adam apply to us today?

Although deeply distorted by sin, the original mandate to take dominion is still a mandate. It is a part of God's original intention. Everything we are trying to do, by the power of the gospel of Jesus Christ, is to get back to God's original intention for our lives. God has created men—under His authority, on His behalf, as His representatives manifesting His character—to take dominion.

In what ways do you see the distortion of manhood in the world around you?

In what ways can you contribute to helping our culture regain a biblical understanding of manhood?

There are two words in Genesis 2 that give clarity on the meaning of dominion: *work* and *keep* (Genesis 2:15). The primary role of every man in every area of his life is summarized in those two words. Every man is called to work and keep. That is godly dominion.

What are some areas of life that God is calling you to take dominion?
How are you stewarding those responsibilities?

End your time together by praying for one another. Remind the group to complete the five days of personal study prior to the next group meeting.

Working & Keeping

Read Genesis 2:8-15.

There are two words in Genesis 2 that give clarity on the meaning of dominion: *work* and *keep* (Genesis 2:15). When you think about *work*, think about a plow. A plow is used to cultivate the earth, to turn up the soil and prepare the ground for seed. Although modern inventions have made plowing easier than ever, plowing is hard work; it's cultivating the earth so that what is planted will grow. That is a great picture of what it means for a man to work.

Plowing is a selfless and thankless task. It's not just hard work, it's sweaty work. Yet, plowing is the work every man should be devoted to—not to tend a garden, but to work hard for the sake of others—to sweat and toil, to cultivate and nurture everything and everyone God has put under his charge. As a man, you were created to work in that way.

Every man should wake up in the morning and imagine a plow in his hand, ready to work. This is God's calling. Under your leadership, things should grow and thrive.

When you think about *keeping*, think about a sword. To keep is to watch, guard, and protect. What God has put under your charge should not only grow and thrive; it should be cared for and protected. God has created every man to be a guardian, a protector, and a defender. He is called to stand in the watchtower and watch and to take up his sword and fight.

Working and keeping are at the very core of manhood. God models both for us in the garden. He creates us in His image so we might reflect His glory by doing the same. When you work and keep as a man living under the authority of Jesus Christ and filled with the Holy Spirit, you bear the image of God and begin to lay a foundation for manhood.

Think about plowing a large field with a hand-held instrument. What would that kind of work demand and require?

In what ways do you need those same qualities in your life right now?

Plowing requires cultivating the ground so that something might grow. In what ways does manhood require you to do work that no one else sees but that will bear fruit much later?

Every man is called to keep—to be a protector and defender. In what specific areas of your life do you see the need for "keeping"?

What specific examples of working and keeping can you think of from the Bible or men you have known?

The First Domain: Flesh

Read Titus 1:1-16.

The areas in which God calls a man to take dominion are called *domains*. You can't give a man dominion without giving him a domain. This is where the structure of the book of Titus helps us. The three chapters of Titus give us three domains of every man: his church, his family, and his work. But all three chapters of Titus show us another area in which every man must take dominion: his own flesh.

After Paul told Titus to find good men and put them in leadership, he told Titus what to look for. Listen to how he described the men the church needs:

> *If anyone is above reproach, the husband of one wife, and his children are believers and not open to the charge of debauchery or insubordination. For an overseer, as God's steward, must be above reproach. He must not be arrogant or quick-tempered or a drunkard or violent or greedy for gain, but hospitable, a lover of good, self-controlled, upright, holy, and disciplined. He must hold firm to the trustworthy word as taught, so that he may be able to give instruction in sound doctrine and also to rebuke those who contradict it.*
> **TITUS 1:6–9**

Apart from the direct reference to a man having self-control, there are multiple references to things that demand self-control. A godly man must be able to control his pride, his temper, his drinking, and his flesh. A man cannot be a leader until he learns to take dominion over himself.

Taking dominion over your flesh is not just about fighting against sin. We will never gain any victory over sin unless we truly believe walking with Jesus is better than living in sin. We should long for the life, joy, peace, and blessing that come when we walk with Jesus. Our primary motive is always more of Jesus.

The qualifications for an elder in Titus 1 function as a list of what it means to be a godly man. As you read over that passage, where do you see the need for self-control?

In what specific areas of a man's life does he need to practice self-control?

How have you see the lack of self-control affect your life or the life of someone you know?

How can a lack of self-control over the flesh affect every other area of your life?

What are some practical areas in which you need to take dominion over your flesh?

The Second Domain: Church

Read Ephesians 5:22-28.

Paul wrote Titus to help him fix a church that was in massive turmoil (Titus 1:5). The primary cause of turmoil was the presence of useless, ungodly, and rebellious men (1:10–16). And their actions were tearing apart entire families (1:11). The first thing Paul told Titus to do was find godly men—those who have cultivated self-control—and put them in leadership in the church. Even though the families were suffering, Paul did not say the first step was to fix the families but to fix the church. The first place he called godly men into action was the church.

The church is the body of Christ. The church is the bride of Christ. The church is the house of God. The church is the family of God. God uses those metaphors so that we might understand His love for the church and to stir up our love for the church. And "church" is not just a reference to all believers everywhere but to specific believers in local assemblies in which the body, bride, house, and family are manifested.

This Bible is clear, you cannot say you love Christ if you do not love His bride. You cannot say you are serving Christ if you are not an active part of His body. If you are not sacrificially attending, serving, and supporting a local church, you cannot become the man God wants you to be. God has set His church as the primary place where He works in and through men.

The local church is not only the primary place where a man learns to be a Christian, but it is also the primary place where a man learns to be a man. There, surrounded by generations of godly men, he learns about himself and his God. Find a church and make it a priority. Give it your greatest effort. Serve it, love it, and protect it. Work and keep it.

You cannot become the man God wants you to be without involvement in a local church. Why would this be true?

The church is called the "bride of Christ." What does that tell us about how God feels about His church? How should we feel about His church?

What role does the local church play in your life? Are you treating your local church like Christ would want you to treat His bride? How could you better work and keep in your local church?

In what ways can the local church help you learn how to be a man?

How would the lack of church involvement negatively affect your life? How would active engagement in a local church affect your life?

The Third Domain: Family

Read Titus 2:1-15.

Your next domain is your family. If you are young and/or single, don't skip this section. This also includes you.

One of the reasons a young man must learn to take dominion over his flesh, as well as sacrificially lead in his church, is that both of those things prepare him to take dominion in the home. When a father allows his family to make other things more important than the church, the father undermines the primary training ground for his family. God has given us the local church as the means to train us in how to love those in our family— this is the point of Titus 2. And then, God calls us to go home to work and keep.

When a man comes home from work, he must continue to work. This can be challenging. The temptation is to come home from work and totally check out, especially if your job is demanding and you have worked hard all day. But God has called you to take dominion in the home. He has entrusted you with your family. Your family is not anyone else's responsibility—it is your responsibility, and it is your domain.

Taking dominion in the home demands the constant use of the plow and the sword. Serve your wife. Serve your children. Love, honor, and serve your parents. Be the hardest worker at home. Give yourself sacrificially every single day for the good of your family. And it's not just about working hard and providing. It's about doing the hard work of loving, leading, and serving at home. A woman will not despise the idea of godly dominion if she sees this manifested in the way the men in her life love, serve, and help at home.

Why do men often feel more equipped to lead at work than at home?

Why is the work at home so often more difficult?

In what ways do you feel insecure and insufficient to do the work God has called you to do at home?

In what practical ways can you better serve, love, and lead those in your home?

If you are single, how can you serve and love your family in order to become the man God has called you to be?

The Fourth Domain: World

Read Titus 3:1-15.

Finally, every man must take dominion in the workplace. Titus transitions from life in the church (Titus 1) to life in the home (Titus 2), to life in the workplace (Titus 3). Titus 3 begins with these words to employees: "Remind them to be submissive to rulers and authorities, to be obedient, to be ready for every good work, to speak evil of no one, to avoid quarreling, to be gentle, and to show perfect courtesy toward all people" (vv. 1-2). Notice that to be a godly man at work, you must learn through the ministry of the local church and the ministry in the home how to obey, work, deal with conflict, and be kind.

The workplace is where a man displays to a lost world self-sacrificing, loving, and godly dominion. It is where a man shows the world God's original intention. Paul says, "Whatever you do, work heartily, as for the Lord and not for men" (Colossians 3:23). No one should be a harder worker, a better employee, or a better boss than a man who follows Jesus. You should work harder, sacrifice more, and lead more honestly and graciously than anyone else. In doing so, you are not only seeking your good and the good of those under your charge, but you are also seeking to glorify God through your work ethic.

The only reason the world has a problem with the idea of manly dominion is that they have not seen dominion as God intended it. To use your plow and sword in your domains is to work hard, sweat, toil, and sacrifice for the good of those under your charge. It is about manifesting the very death of Christ for the good of others. Taking dominion is about displaying the gospel in the way you die to yourself and live for the good of others. It's about seeing the way sin has distorted God's original intention. It is about manifesting the glory of God. It is about having our manhood redeemed. And that is where we go next.

In what ways do our jobs teach us how to work and keep?

If you are a student or retired, what work has God still called you to do, and how can you take dominion in that?

How can working and keeping be a testimony to those at work?

How have you see the lack of a strong work ethic affect men?

Are there areas in your life where you need to be working harder? If so, what are they and what changes do you need to make?

Gospel

Group Study

START

Welcome to week 2 of The Titus Ten.
Use this page to get the conversation going.

Last week, we looked at what it means for men to exercise the call to dominion. This week, we will be talking about and applying the gospel to manhood.

What was one key takeaway from last week's group teaching or personal study?

What is one way the gospel applies to our manhood?

When Paul wrote to Titus and gave him instructions on how to navigate all the dysfunction in the church at Crete, he told him to begin by dealing with the rebellious men. Paul wrote, "For there are many who are insubordinate, empty talkers, and deceivers" (Titus 1:10). These men were dividing the church, disrupting families, and destroying the church's effectiveness and witness. And most of these actions were caused by a group Paul referred to as "the circumcision party" (1:10). The root issue in Crete was not just the rebellious men but a misunderstood and misapplied gospel taught by rebellious men. The gospel is the only remedy that has the power to fully address our broken manhood.

WATCH

Use this page to take notes as you watch video session 2.

To access the teaching sessions,
use the instructions in the back
of your Bible study book.

DISCUSS

Use this page to facilitate the group discussion.

Every action we take, whether big or small, positive or negative, has a rippling effect. Every decision, every word, every step, every moment will have some influence on your life and the lives of others.

What are some examples of the ripple effects of sin in the Bible?

How have you seen the ripple effects of sin in your life? How have you seen sin—your own or that of others—negatively affect you and others?

There is no place where we see the ripple effects of one decision more than in the garden of Eden. In one moment, Adam and Eve believed there was something better than life with God. And with one decision, as Adam and Eve rebelled against a holy God and sin entered the world, everything was broken.

What is the difference between sin and brokenness?

Brokenness is not the same as sin. Sin is rebellion against a holy God. Brokenness is the effect of that rebellion in our lives and the world around us. When we see the brokenness in our lives, our marriages, our relationships, our world—we are seeing the ripple effects of sin. Sin brought brokenness into every area of life, including our manhood.

Read Titus 2:11-14 together.

The root issue in the letter to Titus wasn't sinful and rebellious men, but a misunderstood and misapplied gospel taught by rebellious men.

The true gospel can be summarized in the following way:

1. Sin has enslaved you.
2. God is pursuing you.
3. Jesus came to redeem you.
4. Salvation saves and restores you.

In what ways could a misunderstanding of the gospel negatively affect your life?

Why is the gospel is the foundation for everything?

What are some specific ways the gospel speaks to our manhood?

If you get everything in life right but get the gospel wrong, you have nothing right. The gospel forms everything and brings clarity to everything. The gospel changes everything and is the foundation of everything. The gospel is the only way you will know how to take what is broken and put it back together—especially manhood. The gospel is the only path out of a distorted view of manhood and back to God's original intention.

End your time together by praying for one another. Remind the group to complete the five days of personal study prior to the next group meeting.

Manhood Broken

Read Genesis 3:1-19.

Before Eve ever ate the forbidden fruit, Adam had already lost the battle for both of them. God told Adam and Eve to take dominion over the earth (Genesis 1:28), a commission in which Adam was called to be the leader and Eve was called to be the indispensable helper (2:18-25). Adam's responsibility was to work and keep. God equipped Adam with a plow and a sword and called him—in a life of selfless love—to cultivate, grow, and protect everything under his charge.

But in the garden, before Eve was tempted, Adam put down his plow and sword.

While the Serpent had a conversation with Eve, deceiving her with his words, Adam stood by and did nothing. And then, Adam dared to blame Eve for the sin. In a sense, the original sin was not Eve eating from the fruit but Adam failing to care for her soul and defend her from the Serpent. And that is a crystal-clear picture of the brokenness of manhood.

At the very core, the brokenness of manhood always comes down to the plow and the sword. When a man is self-willed and not living under the rule of God, he misuses his plow and sword. This primarily happens in one of two ways: aggression or passivity. Some men pick up their plows and swords and use them to aggressively dominate and control. Other men lay down their plows and swords and passively watch as those under their care are harassed and abused. Adam did both. He stood there passively while Eve was tempted and then quickly shifted the blame to Eve in an act of self-centered aggression. And that, is broken manhood.

Where was Adam when Satan deceived Eve?

How did Adam fail to take dominion in that moment? What should he have done?

How did Adam's failure effect Eve and all of mankind?

In many ways, Adam's failure in that moment is a picture of the lack of dominion that so many men struggle with. How have you, like Adam, failed to take dominion when you should have?

How does a man misuse his plow and sword when he is not controlled by the Spirit of God? How have you seen that happen?

Manhood Redeemed & Restored

Read Titus 2:11-14; 3:3-7.

Brokenness can only be put together by the gospel of Jesus Christ. The gospel is not just good news for the future; the gospel is good news for today. It is not just a guide to lead us to heaven later but a guide to lead us into life now. When we believe the good news of the gospel and choose to trust and follow Jesus, God begins to lead us out of our broken manhood.

The book of Titus reveals how the gospel affects every area of our lives. In the forty-six verses of this little book, we have two of the most beautiful gospel passages in all of the New Testament. The placement of these passages within the book is significant.

In chapter 2, after giving practical instruction to the men and women of the church, telling them how they should live as the people of God, Paul reminded them of the gospel. Then in chapter 3, after instructing them how to live for Christ in the work-place, Paul reminded them of the gospel. Why? The only way we become the people God intended us to become and live the way God calls us to live is by having our lives deeply rooted in the gospel. You can only become a godly man when your life is built on the foundation of the gospel.

These two passages give us a basic understanding of the gospel and its implications for our lives. They show us the path to a restored and redeemed manhood and remind us that the gospel is essential to every area of our lives.

Reread those two gospel passages carefully. What stands out to you the most?

How is the gospel good news for the future?

How is the gospel good news for today?

How do these passages show that the only way back to a restored manhood is through the gospel?

Why does it matter that we build our daily lives on the gospel?

The Gospel

Read Ephesians 2:1-10.

Titus 2:11-14 and Titus 3:3-7 (like Ephesians 2:1-10) show us four gospel truths that lead us to a restored manhood.

First, sin has enslaved you. You were born spiritually dead. As a result, you are a broken person at your very core. Every man is deeply and painfully broken. There are no exceptions. All of us were once foolish, disobedient, deceived, and enslaved (Titus 3:3). At your very core, having been born in sin and under the bondage of the enemy, you are deeply broken (Ephesians 2:1–3).

Second, God is pursuing you. We have a God who is good, loving, kind, and gracious (Titus 3:4). As those who have rebelled against God and rejected Him, we are under the righteous wrath of God. We deserve eternal separation from Him. But as God's creation, we are cared for by God. He wants to see us saved and restored, and He is pursuing us to that end. This is such good news because none of us would pursue God if left to ourselves (Romans 3:10-18).

Third, Jesus came to redeem you. God displays His grace and pursuit through the appearance of Jesus Christ. To *redeem* means to release a captive, like a prisoner or a slave, through the payment of ransom. Jesus came to purchase us with His very blood and to free us from the bondage of sin. Through Christ, we can be saved from sin and from the just wrath of God.

Finally, salvation restores you. Jesus did not just come to save you from hell; He came to restore your true identity in Him. Salvation is a present-tense reality in which you choose to trust and follow Jesus daily. As you do, God takes you further down the path of restoration.

For these truths to be applied to you, you must choose to trust and follow Jesus. Not just once, but for a lifetime. You must acknowledge your sin, trust Jesus alone as the payment for your sin, and ask Him to save you. The only way to become the man God has called you to be is to trust and follow Jesus.

Do you believe that without Jesus you are a slave to sin? How do you see that truth manifested in your life?

God is pursuing you. If you hunger or thirst for God, that is evidence God is coming after you. How hungry would you say you are for God?

Are you absolutely confident in your relationship with Jesus? Have you trusted Jesus alone as the payment for your sins and asked Him to save you? Explain.

Could you clearly explain the gospel to someone else? If you are doing this study in a small group, practice sharing a simple gospel message with one another.

Following Jesus into True Manhood

Read Romans 8:28-39.

As those who have been saved by God, how do we begin to walk the path toward restored manhood? Simply put: we follow Jesus. Jesus is called the Second Adam (1 Corinthians 15:45-49). Jesus, Son of God and Son of Man, did what Adam could not do. He took His plow and sword and used them perfectly. He lived a life of love, humility, self-sacrifice, and service. Jesus is the model for true manhood. He is the man we long to be. He is the man God has called us to be like. He is the man those around us need us to be. And because of the glorious news of the gospel, He is the man whose image God is conforming us into.

God saves you so that He might then conform you into the image of Jesus (Romans 8:29). This happens as we make the choice to submit ourselves daily to the lordship of Jesus, seek to be filled with the Spirit of Jesus, and strive to live out the life of Jesus. In other words, as we live out the gospel in our daily lives, our manhood is restored.

Sin isn't the only thing that has a ripple effect—so does Christlikeness. The man you long to be, the man God desires for you to be, the man your family needs you to be, is the man God is going to make you into, one decision at a time. It is Jesus alone who can lead you in a life of true manhood each day. And that begins with the first decision to trust and follow Him.

Jesus, unlike Adam, used His plow and sword perfectly. What are some ways Jesus perfectly used His plow and sword?

In what specific ways do you see Jesus as a model of true manhood?

What does it look like to submit to the lordship of Jesus every day?

Would you say your life reflects that you have chosen to trust and follow Jesus? Why or why not?

Choosing to trust and follow Jesus into a restored manhood can feel overwhelming. What are practical steps you can take to more faithfully trust and follow Jesus today?

Coming out from the Crowd

Read Matthew 7:24-27.

When Jesus went up to a mountain to deliver His longest recorded sermon, the Sermon on the Mount, the audience consisted of two distinct groups of people: the crowd and the disciples. Matthew 5:1-2 says, "Seeing the crowds, he went up on the mountain, and when he sat down, his disciples came to him. And he opened his mouth and taught them." There was a large crowd of people and a small group of disciples. And although the large crowd was present and listening, Jesus seemed to be speaking to the smaller crowd. He was preaching to His disciples.

The "crowd" was a group of people who liked Jesus. He fascinated them, and His words and actions intrigued them. Wherever Jesus went, they followed. The crowd was aware of His healing powers and miraculous works, and they wanted to get in on that. They were caught up in the excitement and didn't want to miss anything. They are called "the crowd" because there were many of them. There always are.

And then there were the disciples. This was a smaller group of people who didn't just like being around Jesus but decided to trust and follow Jesus. So, when Jesus sat down on a mountain to teach about the way to live in the kingdom of God, He spoke to those who were part of the kingdom—His disciples. The crowd was listening, but the sermon was not for them.

Local churches are filled with men who part of the crowd. They are present but not committed. They listen but they do not respond. From the outside, they may appear to be disciples, but a closer look will reveal that there is little love and desire for Jesus.

Nothing matters more than making sure you are a disciple and not just a member of the crowd. But it takes courage to step out of the larger crowd and into the smaller group of disciples. This is the starting place of a godly life—the foundation. And now is the time. Don't settle for just being around Jesus; trust and follow Him with your whole heart.

What is the difference between a man in the crowd and a man who is a disciple?

What does our reading from Matthew 7:24-27 tell us about the lives of those who have chosen to become disciples of Jesus?

How does Jesus invite people out of the crowd into discipleship?

What does it look like to just be a part of the crowd? What does it look like to be an actual disciple of Jesus?

Are you confident that you are a disciple and not just a member of the crowd? Explain.

The Titus Ten

Week 3

Identity

Group Study

START

Having walked through foundational ideas like dominion and the importance of getting the gospel right, this week we're going to turn our attention to identity.

What was the most significant lesson or thought you had during last week's group or personal study? Share with the group.

Fill in the blanks: My name is _____, and I am a _____.

The first blank is easy. You have a name. You didn't choose it. It was given to you. You've had it your whole life. It's what people call you. You don't have to think about it. You don't have to hesitate when people ask you. You've said it a million times.

The second blank might be a little more difficult. There are a lot of things that could fill it. The first thought you might have when you look at the second blank is, *Where do I start?* Sometimes you may feel like you are an overwhelming number of things—a lot of different things to a lot of different people at a lot of different times.

Despite the difficulty, our ability to clearly and quickly fill in that second blank is as important as the first one. The first blank is just your name. The second blank is your identity. Or at least, it should be.

WATCH

Use this page to take notes as you watch video session 3.

To access the teaching sessions,
use the instructions in the back
of your Bible study book.

DISCUSS

Use this page to facilitate the group discussion.

Everyone has an identity. Whether you realize it or not, your identity is most formed by words others have said to you, phrases that begin with words like, "You are," "You will never be," or "You are just like." These often careless words can define us and leave many of us with an inner monologue that continues to reinforce a false identity. They can become a curse. And we all have them.

Why is it important to have a clear sense of identity?

What are the consequences of not being clear on your identity?

Every one of us has had defining, and often hurtful, words spoken to us. These words often shape our identity. What words like this have been spoken to you? What shaping effect have they had on you?

All of us have an inner monologue—an inner voice always talking to us. When you hear that voice, what does it say about you and your identity?

When we trust and follow Jesus, He makes us into new creations. He redefines us. And on the pathway to a restored manhood, we must continue to allow our identity to be formed, not by what others have said about us but what God says about us. Then, the curse of false words is replaced by the blessing of a true identity in Jesus. You must have a clear identity formed by who you are in Christ.

How can the gospel redefine you and give you a new identity?

Read Ephesians 1:3-14 and take note of everything it says about your identity in Christ. Which of these is most meaningful to you?

How does the gospel speak to the various false identities we've been given or we've taken on ourselves?

Many of a man's struggles are directly related to his lack of a clear identity. If you do not have a clear identity, you will allow your past, your failures, your success, or the words and the expectations of others define you. Your life will feel like a treadmill of uncertainty that never stops. It's exhausting. You must settle the issue of identity, and you do that by allowing the gospel to redefine you.

End your time together by praying for one another. Remind the group to complete the five days of personal study prior to the next group meeting.

You Are a Servant

Read Titus 1:1-4.

When it comes to understanding true manhood and becoming godly men, four primary words must become your core identity: You are a servant, a son, a friend, and a lover.

When Jesus invited people to Himself, He simply said, "Follow me" (Matthew 4:19; John 1:43). Following Him demands faith and repentance. To follow Jesus, you must believe He alone is the way, truth, and life (John 14:6). Then, as a response of faith, you must be willing to completely submit your life to Him. You must be willing to become a slave of Jesus Christ. And as counterintuitive as it seems, true manhood and true freedom begin when you choose to become a slave.

This is why Paul began his letter to Titus like he so often began his letters: "Paul, a servant of God and an apostle of Jesus Christ" (Titus 1:1).

What does it mean to be a slave? "A slave is one who is in a permanent relation of servitude to another, his will being altogether consumed in the will of the other. Generally, one serving, bound to serve, in bondage."[1] There are five parallels between biblical Christianity and first-century slavery: exclusive ownership, complete submission, singular devotion, total dependence, and personal accountability.

Everything in our lives begins with the initial and then daily decision to allow our wills to be consumed with the will of Christ. This is the greatest battle of our lives—the battle to submit to Jesus Christ and allow Him to lead and control our lives. As a follower of Christ, you are a slave. And there is nothing more freeing than being a slave to Jesus.

You don't have to be afraid of being fully surrendered to Jesus. You don't have to be your own man. You don't have to chart your own course. You don't have to figure everything out. You just have to be a submissive servant of Jesus Christ. You must surrender completely to Him and embrace being a slave of Jesus Christ.

When you think about the idea of becoming a slave of Jesus Christ, what initially comes to your mind?

Look at the definition of what it means to be a slave. What part of that would be most challenging for you?

Why do men so often find it hard to surrender their will and allow Jesus to lead and control their lives? Is this challenging for you? Why or why not?

Why is it necessary for every person to begin his relationship with Jesus as a submissive slave? Why is it necessary for every person to continue his relationship with Jesus as a submissive slave?

How could living this way being joyful and freeing?

You Are a Son

Read Mark 1:9-13.

At the baptism of Jesus, God the Father opened up the heavens and declared to His Son, so that everyone there could hear, "You are my beloved Son; with you I am well pleased" (Mark 1:11). With those words, the Father gave the Son the three things every son needs most from his father: acceptance, affection, and affirmation. There will always be a void in a man's life unless he receives those three things from his father.

Unfortunately, many men never hear words like that from their earthly father. And as much as men try to act like they are okay without those things, they are not. The lack of those three things leaves wounds in the heart of every man. Although those wounds can be partially healed by a healthy relationship with a man's earthly father, it can only truly be healed by a healthy relationship with our heavenly Father.

Because of your union with Christ, you are adopted into the family of God and have become a child of God. As a result, your heavenly Father says to you, "You are Mine. I love you. I'm proud of you." You find in Him the acceptance, affection, and affirmation you long for. This may sound strange, but you have to allow yourself to hear those words spoken to you. No matter what anyone else has ever said to you, if you are a child of God, God loves you and is proud of you. God sees you as His son. God is pleased with you.

Something about that truth touches us deeply. Our tendency may be to quickly move on and ignore what God is trying to do in us. Often we feel unable to look at the Father and allow Him to say those words to us. But we must stop and allow the fatherly love of God to touch us deeply. We need to hear those words and believe them. You are His beloved son.

In your relationship with your earthly father, did you receive acceptance, affection, and affirmation? How did this affect you, negatively or positively?

In what ways does being a child of God form your identity and make you feel more confident?

When we come to Jesus, we are adopted into God's family and made His sons. How does that reality encourage you?

What are the real, daily implications of knowing you are a son of God?

How can the reality of sonship make you feel more settled and less like you need to earn God's favor?

You Are a Friend

Read John 15:9-17.

As you grow in your relationship with Christ, you remain both a slave and a son. You are a submissive slave and a beloved son. Both of these phrases communicate something different about the nature of your identity in Christ. And from there, we can begin to see ourselves as true friends.

In John 15, as Jesus taught His disciples about their need to continually abide in Him, He made an amazing statement. Jesus said, "I do not call you servants anymore, because a servant doesn't know what his master is doing. I have called you friends, because I have made known to you everything I have heard from my Father" (v. 15 CSB). Jesus calls you a friend.

This progression in our relationship with God is important. In a servant-master relationship, the master is clearly above the slave. The master tells the slave what to do, and the slave does it. There are no questions, no discussion, no debate.

In a father-son relationship, the father is still above the son, but there is a relational closeness. There is love. There is affection. There is the communication. There is still authority, but there is also relationship.

But Jesus goes beyond the father-son relationship and says He longs for friendship. The relationship of a friend moves from an authoritative, top-down relationship, to a side-by-side relationship. In a friendship, you talk more openly, share more honestly, and simply enjoy being together. You have a kind of closeness with a friend that you do not have with a father.

Jesus is inviting us into friendship. What an amazing thought. God is still the master of our lives. God is still a loving Father who guides us in the way of wisdom. But He also invites us to walk with Him, enjoy His company, and enjoy an intimacy that only friends can experience. He enjoys your company and wants to spend time with you. He does not just want to be your Lord and your Father; He wants to be your friend.

How do master-servant, father-son, and friend relationships differ?

What would you talk with a friend about that you would not talk to a boss or your father about?

When Jesus invites us into friendship with Him, what do you think He wants in that relationship? What would make this distinct from the master-servant relationship?

Does anything about your relationship with God feel like friendship? Why or why not?

What would make it challenging to enter a friendship with God?

You Are a Lover

Read John 15:15-19.

In a book on manhood, this is a difficult concept to understand. But it is a concept we must understand to have the kind of identity we need to be the men God has called us to be.

When Jesus saw Peter after His resurrection—and Peter's denial—Jesus only asked Peter one question: "Do you love me?" When Jesus asked this question, He used two different words for love. The first two times Jesus asked Peter, He used the word *agape*, which is a more general word for unconditional love. But the third time, Jesus used the word *phileo*, which refers to a more relational, affectionate, and intimate love. What was Jesus doing? He was calling Peter into deeper love.

Jesus calls every man into a deeper, more intimate, more passionate love relationship. Jesus wants you to fall in love with Him. After all, the first and greatest commandment is to have a passionate, all-consuming love for God (Matthew 22:37). The continual call of God on every man of God is to love Him more and more. And the reality is, if a man does not understand how to love God, he will never learn how to love his wife, his children, or his neighbors. You were created to be a passionate lover, and the truest men are those who love the most deeply and passionately—starting with your love for God.

Seeing yourself as a servant is the starting place of a relationship with Jesus. The first call of Jesus is to follow Him. We respond by submitting ourselves to Him as slaves. But this is just the starting place. As we come to know Jesus more, He calls us into a deeper relationship. He is calling you into sonship, friendship, and intimate love. He is calling you to move toward intimacy. And as we move in that direction toward God, we can move in that direction toward others.

As strange as this might sound, it is simple a call to obey the first and primary commandment: to love God with all your heart, soul, and strength. You were created to fall in love with God.

What does it mean to love God with all of your heart, soul, and strength?

Does that kind of love characterize your relationship with God? How can you know?

Read Psalm 42:1-2. You would not say those words to your boss, your dad, or a friend. You would only say those words to someone you passionately love and long for. Does your relationship with God feel that way? Why or why not?

If you never learn to love God this way, you will not be able to love your wife and children this way. Why is this true?

What do you need to do to cultivate more passionate love for God?

PERSONAL STUDY 5

The Vicious Cycle

Read Ephesians 1:3-14.

If you do not understand your own identity, you can't be the man, husband, father, leader, or church member God wants you to be. It is your knowledge, experience, intimacy, and security in Jesus that allows you to be the man God calls you to be in every area of life. Your identity can also save you from a vicious and exhausting cycle.

If your identity is not solidly in Jesus, you will spend your life controlled by three things: comparison, competition, and coveting. These three things, deep in the heart of every man, will control you unless your identity is firmly rooted in Jesus.

You will continually compare yourself, your family, your job, your finances, and your gifts with other men around you. Comparison always leads to coveting. This is a subtle but certain shift. As you compare your life to someone else's, you will begin to covet what they have. Our comparing makes us think that what others have is better than what we have. Most likely, it's not. Every person we compare ourselves to has just as many issues and problems as we do.

Comparing and coveting always lead to competing. You know this is true. Men love to compete—not just on the field but in life. Many men are driven by their desire to have more than other men. To have a better job, a better car, a nicer home, or a more successful child. When you think about it, it's a pitiful cycle. But it's the certain cycle of every man who does not have his identity settled and established in Jesus Christ.

Let Jesus redefine you every moment of every day. Remind yourself of who you are. Immerse yourself in His Word so that He is the One who whispers your true identity in your ear. Then, remind yourself. Tell yourself all the time. Make sure your inner monologue is not filled with false curses but true blessing. And continue to grow in that reality until the Lord takes you home. As you do, you'll feel yourself becoming a more whole and solid man.

How does a settled and secure identity in Jesus affect every other area of your life?

When do you feel the tendency to live in comparison with other men? How does that affect you?

Read Exodus 20:17. Has coveting been a struggle for you? Why do we easily covet what we do not have?

Men love to compete. Without even realizing it, we often find ourselves competing with other men in many areas of our life. What makes us do that? How could that negatively affect you?

What are practical steps you can take to continue to be redefined by Jesus? What specific truths about your identity in Jesus do you need to keep reminding yourself of? What are your areas of greatest struggle, and how can you combat that with your true identity?

The Titus Ten

Assignments

Group Study

START

Welcome to week 4 of The Titus Ten.
Use this page to get the conversation going.

Last week, we considered an all important question: Who am I? This week, we will consider a question that flows from it: What has God called me to do?

What is one truth that resonated with you from last week's group session or personal study?

How does who we are in Christ inform the things that God has called us to do?

Once your identity becomes clear, you must get clarity on your assignments. Identity answers the question, "Who am I?" Assignments answer the question, "What has God called me to do?" Being able to answer these two crucial questions is an essential task for all men who are seeking to embrace God's best for their manhood.

WATCH

Use this page to take notes as you watch video session 4.

To access the teaching sessions,
use the instructions in the back
of your Bible study book.

DISCUSS

Use this page to facilitate the group discussion.

What is the difference between your identity and your assignments?

Identity never changes. Assignments often change. Identity must be held tightly. Assignments must be held loosely. Identity is about being. Assignments are about doing. Identity and assignments are distinct but inseparable. Your identity is the foundation for understanding and accomplishing your assignments. And if you do not understand your identity first, then your assignments will become your identity. Many struggles come in a man's life when he does not know the difference between his identity and his assignments.

Why are identity and assignments "distinct but inseparable"?

What are some ways men find identity in their assignments? Why is it so important to make sure you do not find your identity in your assignments?

Read Titus 1:1. How do we see the distinction between Paul's identity and assignments?

As Paul began his letter to Titus, he gave both his identity and his assignment. He said, "Paul, a servant of God and an apostle of Jesus Christ" (Titus 1:1). In those simple words, he showed he understood the difference between his identity and his assignments. His identity was a servant of God. His assignment was to be an apostle of God. A servant is who he was; being an apostle is what he did.

Much of Paul's confidence and effectiveness in his life and ministry resulted from his clear understanding of the distinct and inseparable nature of identity and assignments. Our confidence and effectiveness will come from the same clarity.

Most men do not think carefully about these two things. As a result, they just move thoughtlessly through life. Where do you see that temptation in your life?

How would your life potentially change if you had clarity about who God has called you to be and what God has called you to do?

True manhood demands clarity on both our identity and assignments. You must continue to resist the urge to just exist, to thoughtlessly move from one thing to the next, and to just passively let life happen. You must see what matters most in life and give yourself fully to those things while ruthlessly eliminating what does not matter. Life is too short to be vague about your assignments.

What are your assignments? How can we support one another in pursing our God given assignments?

End your time together by praying for one another. Remind the group to complete the five days of personal study prior to the next group meeting.

Clarifying Your Assignments

Read 1 Corinthians 3:1-9.

The idea of God-given assignments may be new to you. Because of that, clarifying these assignments might take some time, thought, prayer, and conversation with others. But getting clarity on this is essential to your effectiveness.

A God-given assignment is anyone God has entrusted to you and anything God has called you to do. For instance, being a husband to your wife is your God-given assignment, not anyone else's. Being a father to your children is your God-given assignment, not anyone else's. Your ministry within your local church, your job, school, and with your grandchildren are all God-given assignments.

Your assignments are the responsibilities or people that have been entrusted to your care. To think about it in terms of your true manhood, in what areas of your life have you been called to use your plow and your sword? What are your domains? Don't just think in vague terms; be specific.

Right now, don't worry about the priority of these things. Just begin by making a list of everyone God has entrusted to you and everything God has called you to do. Think about it this way: What are the things in life that, if you neglected them, would indicate you had not been faithful to the Lord? You might be surprised by what is on this list. You might also be surprised by what is not on this list.

EVERYONE   **EVERYTHING**

What is a God-given assignment?

Is there are anything on your list that you had not thought about being a God-given assignment? Explain.

How do you think seeing these things as God-given assignments will help you steward them with more care and diligence?

Are there things you are spending a lot of time on that are *not* on your list? What does that indicate?

Take a few moments to discuss this with someone close to you. Ask him what he perceives are your God-given assignments. Did he think of anything that should be on your list that wasn't?

Walking Carefully in Your Assignments

Read Ephesians 5:15-17.

The Christian life demands something we don't often want to give: careful thought. But walking with Jesus demands it. We will never live a purposeful, productive, and priority-driven life without careful thought. And there is no area in which this is more true than the area of our God-given assignments.

This is the kind of thought the apostle Paul was calling for when he said, "Look carefully then how you walk, not as unwise but as wise, making the best use of the time, because the days are evil. Therefore, do not be foolish, but understand what the will of the Lord is" (Ephesians 5:15–17). It is what Solomon meant when he said, "Let your eyes look directly forward, and your gaze be straight before you. Ponder the path of your feet; then all your ways will be sure" (Proverbs 4:25–26). The word *ponder* means "to give careful thought and consideration."

Prioritizing your life matters, but learning what is priority is not simple. The decisions we make every day about our priorities are not always easy. And yet, we must make these decisions. If we don't take this kind of thoughtful approach to life, we will inevitably waste our lives. A thoughtful approach to life is complicated, but these complications are actually a blessing because they force us into a more intentional life.

But how do you know what needs priority from week to week? You consider carefully how you walk. You ponder. Before starting the week, you look at your calendar and your assignments, and you plan our week accordingly. You have conversations with those closest to you to determine what areas need the most attention in different seasons. You take the time to make sure your life is driven by your God-given responsibilities.

Why do so many people move through life without much careful thought?

How could taking more time to "ponder" your life, decisions, time, calendar, change your life in positive ways?

How could taking more time to "ponder" disrupt your life in challenging ways?

Why it is essential to think carefully about how you spend your time each week?

Are there any important areas of your life being neglected because you are not being careful about your time or because your priorities are wrong? What changes do you need to make?

Asking the Hard Questions

Read Proverbs 4:25-26.

If you want to live a priority-driven life and faithfully fulfill your God-given assignments, you must ask important and challenging questions like:

- Are any of my God-given assignments suffering due to lack of attention?
- Are there certain things I need to say no or yes to this week?
- Are there any assignments that need more attention right now?
- Are there any assignments I am avoiding right now?
- Are any of my assignments suffering because of the amount of time I am spending on something that is not an assignment?
- Do my priorities and time this week reflect what is most important?

When you take the time to ask questions like these, you ensure that you are not mindlessly living while important things are suffering. They allow you to live a well-ordered and productive life where the things that matter most get the most attention.

Questions like these help you see how to budget your time. Like money, you have a limited amount of time every week. And like money, without a plan, that time will go quickly and you will accomplish less than you would like. So, like with money, if you want that time to be spent wisely and to have enough to accomplish what you need, you make a budget. Instead of being a burden, that budget actually leads to great freedom and a sense of purpose.

Since the priority of our assignments not only change by season but by week, we must ask these questions continually. Ideally, we will ask them each week as we plan for the week ahead. This will ensure that we are continually submitting our will, time, and lives to the direction of the Lord. This forces us to listen to the Lord and make wise decisions. It is learning how to live moment by moment under the guidance of the Spirit of God.

Are you in the habit of asking important questions like these? If not, why not? What keeps you from taking the time to do this?

How could your life change if you asked questions like this regularly? What benefit would it be?

Take time to answer some of those questions now.

What do the answers to those questions reveal?

Share some of your answers with another man you trust. Ask him to help you assess yourself honestly in these areas.

The Priority of the Church

Read 1 Corinthians 12:1-27.

When we begin to think carefully about our assignments, many men neglect to think carefully about the role of the church in their own lives and the lives of their families. Yet, God intended for the local church to have a high place in our priorities.

When Paul wrote to Titus, the church and the homes were in major distress. Yet, the first thing Paul told Titus was to get the church in order—not the home. Even though there were problems in the home (Titus 1:11; 2:1–6), the first priority was the church. Healthy families grow out of healthy churches. The reason for this is simple—if you try to get your home in order without the ministry of the church, your home will never be in order. The church must have a place of priority.

Men, the church is not only the very body of Christ, the church is the bride of Christ. Do you think Jesus cares about the way we treat His bride? Do you think His bride matters to Him? Do you think He passively looks the other way when we disregard His bride? Not only is the health of your family tied to your commitment to the local church, but your walk with Jesus is also tied to your commitment to the local church.

In practical terms, this means making sure you are an identifiable and active member of a local church. In others words, you know you are a member of the church, and the church knows you are a member. You attend regularly, give sacrificially, participate in the church's mission, and have an identifiable area of ministry in which you serve. It means your family knows the local church matters and is a priority. And this is not out of a sense of drudgery or duty but from an awareness that the local church is the body and bride of Christ Himself. You love the church because you love Christ.

Are you actively engaged and committed to a local church? If so, how?
If not, what is keeping you from this?

What role does the local church play in your life? Are you giving it the kind
of attention and time it deserves?

If the church is the bride and body of Christ, what does that tell us about
how God feels about the church? What does that say about how we should
feel about the church?

Why is the local church essential to your life, growth, and progress?

Why is the local church essential to the growth and health of your family?

The Sufficiency of God

Read 2 Corinthians 12:1-10.

When we begin to think carefully about our God-given assignments and how to prioritize them, we might feel both overwhelmed and inadequate. And although no man wants to feel overwhelmed and inadequate, those feelings might actually be a good and healthy first response to what God is calling us into.

The overwhelmed feeling comes from the sense that there is more to do than we have time for. Most men live every day with this feeling. But it is simply not true. The reality is, God has given you enough time to do everything He has called you to do. But God has not given you enough time to do all He has called you to do and a thousand other things.

We are a distracted generations. Our phones often keep our minds preoccupied with something else while in the presence of those who need our attention. To be faithful with our God-given assignments, we must discipline ourselves to be fully present in every moment. Instead of feeling overwhelmed by what needs to be done or what we could be doing, we must be careful to do what is in front of us at the moment.

The feeling of inadequacy is also very real. Most men feel inadequate in many areas of life. A man who is highly successful at work might feel like a failure at home. As a result, he might avoid going home. Men prefer to be in places where they feel like a success. But that feeling of inadequacy is not your enemy   it is actually a gift.

God uses that feeling of inadequacy to drive us to Him. The reality is, you don't have what it takes to faithfully fulfill your God-given assignments. But God does. And your feeling of inadequacy must continually drive you to Him. Don't run away from the areas in which you feel inadequate—stop and thank the Lord for those feelings. Then, ask for His grace, wisdom, and strength to fulfill the assignments. He is sufficient.

Where do you currently feel overwhelmed or inadequate?

Where do you feel that the most? Are there certain areas in which those feelings are more prominent?

When you have those feelings, how do you typically respond? Are you avoiding any areas of responsibility because of those feelings?

From our reading in 2 Corinthians 12:1-10, how did Paul view those feelings?

If you are not sufficient, but God is, how should those feelings continually drive you to Him? Read John 15:5. How does this verse, combined with your feelings of inadequacy, drive you to greater intimacy with Jesus?

The Titus Ten

Authority

Group Study

START

Welcome to week 5 of The Titus Ten.
Use this page to get the conversation going.

Last week, we discussed another essential aspect of biblical manhood: our assignments. This week, we will look at our posture in and toward the world.

What is one key point that stuck with you from last week's study?

Why do you think so many men struggle with passivity?

Men have been called to exercise godly authority for the good and benefit of those entrusted to their care. However, our culture is sliding toward another extreme. There is an epidemic among men that is destroying men, families, churches, and communities at an alarming rate: passivity.

WATCH

Use this page to take notes as you watch video session 5.

To access the teaching sessions,
use the instructions in the back
of your Bible study book.

DISCUSS

Use this page to facilitate the group discussion.

In his 1867 inaugural address at the University of St. Andrews, John Stuart Mill said, "Let not any one pacify his conscience by the delusion that he can do no harm if he takes no part, and forms no opinion. Bad men need nothing more to compass their ends, than that good men should look on and do nothing."[2]

It is not only the things a man does that can have a damaging effect on others; more often, it is what a man fails to do that causes the greatest harm. Could it be that the greatest damage a man can do to himself, his family, his church, and his community, is to do nothing?

How have you seen the effects of men's passivity in your family, your church, and our culture?

Have you seen the effects of passivity in your life? If so, how?

In what areas do you feel most tempted to be passive? Why do you think that is?

Passivity is not a new problem. It has been around since the creation of man. It's what infected Adam when he stood by and allowed the serpent to deceive Eve. Sin came into the world while Adam watched and did nothing. And it seems from that moment on, the enemy knew he could wreak havoc on the world if he could just get men to stand by and do nothing. The enemy wins when men are passive.

Our churches, our families, our nation, and even our lives are constantly under attack. Although we know that, we do not act as if it is true. We so often live as if we are in a time of peace, when in reality, we are in a time of war.

In what ways do you see the assault of the enemy on our churches, families, and our nation?

Read Titus 2:15 and 1 Peter 5:8-9.

What do these verse teach about how to exercise godly authority?

What does it look like to live and model godly authority? Why is this difficult for men to embrace?

Every day, multitudes of men stand by as those around them are spiritually, mentally, emotionally, and even physically assaulted. Some of this is clear and easy to see, while much of it is more subtle. But whether we see the assaults or not, they are there; they are real; and they are destroying the lives of those we love and those who have been entrusted to us. And the passivity of men is often the greatest reason the battles are lost. That is why men must learn to walk in authority.

Who is man you know that stewards his authority well? What have you learned from him?

End your time together by praying for one another. Remind the group to complete the five days of personal study prior to the next group meeting.

PERSONAL STUDY 1

The Most Subtle Assault

Read 1 Peter 5:8-9.

The greatest assault on our lives and the lives of those around us is the most subtle and silent: the spiritual assault of Satan. Many men who would never stand back and watch their wives or children be physically assaulted will stand by while they are being spiritually assaulted.

We tend to think our greatest struggles are with people and situations we can see. But according to Ephesians 6, our greatest battle is an unseen one. You have a very real enemy who has plans to destroy you, your family, your church, and your community. And he is not passive!

Satan is aggressive, subtle, and smart. You must actively resist him. Peter says, "Be sober-minded; be watchful. Your adversary the devil prowls around like a roaring lion, seeking someone to devour. Resist him, firm in your faith, knowing that the same kinds of suffering are being experienced by your brotherhood throughout the world" (1 Peter 5:8–9).

Do you believe that? Do you believe there is a very real enemy out there who is daily assaulting you and that his goal is to devour you? Do you see how this type of spiritual assault could be more eternally damaging than any physical assault?

Peter's use of imagery is interesting. Why would he choose a lion as a picture of how Satan wants to devour us? Because lions are brilliant and fierce hunters. The imagery reveals how dangerous the enemy is. He knows how to hunt and devour. The reality of this demonic lion should make us vigilant.

Satan wins when men are passive. Peter is clear that we can defend ourselves against him if we choose to. Satan does not have to win; his power is real but limited. He wins when we fail to be sober-minded, watchful, and active in resisting him. He fails when we are passive.

How often do you think about the spiritual battle being waged around us? Why is it so difficult to think carefully about this battle?

What would it mean to be more "sober-minded" about this spiritual assault?

In what ways do you see the demonic assault in your life? The lives of those who love? The culture around you?

What does the image of a lion teach us about the assault of Satan?

Why does Satan love when we are passive? How should we respond to his attacks? What weapons has God given us to stand against him?

The Dangers of Passivity

Read Ephesians 6:10-17.

Our tendency toward spiritual passivity allows you and those around you to be assaulted in unimaginable ways with unimaginable consequences. When we, like Adam, stand by and watch while our loved ones are assaulted by the enemy, we fail to walk in our God-given authority. And when that happens, those we love pay the price.

This kind of thing happens every day in moments like this:

- You are struggling with pornography. You resist community and Christian friendship. Instead, you begin to isolate yourself.
- You have a problem with anger that is destroying your family, but you keep it a secret and the problem grows.
- You have an argument with your wife. You feel the hurt and resentment grow. But instead of dealing with it, you ignore it.
- You see ethical issues at work, but you look the other way.
- You hear your children talk back to your wife, but you do nothing.
- Your daughter is pushing the limits in what is acceptable to wear, but you would rather let her leave the house wearing inappropriate clothes than deal with it.
- Your teenage children don't like going to church, so you let them decide.
- There is gossip and division in the church, but you fail to respond for the good of the church.

It is almost always easier to do nothing than to do something. But godly men don't do what is easy, they do what is right.

These types of situations, and many more like them, happen every day in our lives. Our inactivity might seem harmless, but this is exactly how the enemy works. He takes moments like this to get a foothold in our lives. And every time we lose one of those battles, the enemy gains more ground and we lose more ground.

Which of those situations resonate with you?

Are there any situations in life in which your inaction is causing problems?
Explain.

What does our reading from Ephesians 6:10-17 teach us about spiritual warfare?
What weapons do we have to use against the enemy?

When we are told to take our stand, what does that mean practically?

In what areas of your life do you need to more faithfully stand against
the enemy?

Walking in Kingdom Authority

Read Matthew 8:6-9 and Titus 2:15.

Paul left Titus to deal with a very difficult church situation. The church was being ravaged by rebellious men who were tearing the church and families apart. Paul instructed Titus to teach what is right and deal with these rebellious men. Then, after two chapters of instruction, Paul told Titus, "Declare these things; exhort and rebuke with all authority. Let no one disregard you" (Titus 2:15). Paul commanded Titus to walk in authority. We can call this "kingdom authority."

In Luke 9, when Jesus sent out His disciples to proclaim the gospel and heal, He gave them two things: power and authority. Today, Jesus has given all His disciples the same things. In Matthew 28:18-20, He said to go under and in His authority. In Acts 1:8, He said to go out in His power. These are the most important resources we have to be the men God has called us to be.

We can define kingdom authority this way: Kingdom authority is the right and responsibility to act and rule under the king, on behalf of the king, and for the king.

A man of God does not have the right to be passive. We began with the understanding that God has called you to take dominion. In reality, kingdom authority is just the godly expression of dominion. But you cannot walk in authority—the expression of dominion—unless you understand both your identity and your assignments.

There is no better example of kingdom authority than the life of Jesus. In Matthew 8:6-9, we see how Jesus walked in authority and under authority. He was fully submissive to the will of the Father. He was also fully aware of the authority He had been given to do what the father called Him to do.

God has called every man to walk under authority and in authority. We will never be the men God wants us to be without understanding and walking in and under His authority.

When Paul told Titus to walk in authority, what did he mean?
Why did Titus need to walk in authority?

What is "kingdom authority"?

Why is kingdom authority essential to your calling as a man?

Read Matthew 8:6-9. What does this teach us about authority?

What does it mean to walk under authority? What does it mean to walk in authority?

Walking Under Authority

Read John 5:29-30; 17:4-7.

We are often hesitant to talk about walking in authority because we have all seen so many abuses of authority. We might have also heard misunderstandings of kingdom authority within the church. Overly authoritative fathers, pastors, and leaders can make us hesitant to even think about the issue of authority. But the reason authority is most often abused is men try to walk in authority without walking under authority. Every man who tries to walk in authority but not under authority will abuse his authority.

To walk under authority means to walk in complete submission to Jesus. When you choose to trust and follow Jesus, you are saying, "I surrender myself fully to You." And this is not a one-time declaration—this is your daily disposition.

Living as one under authority means you are ready, willing, and eager to be radically obedient to Jesus (John 17:4-7). Like Titus, we must be willing to step into the battle and walk in our authority when God tells us to.

We are not looking for conflict. But when God calls us to step into a battle and walk in God-given authority, we do what He calls us to do.

When we are walking under authority we realize we do not have the right to be passive. Passivity is refusing to live as if you are under the control of Jesus Christ. It is acting as if you are your own man with no regard to the fact that you exist for Jesus. Passivity is not just a bad habit; it is rebellion against God.

The key is this: You cannot be over the things God wants you to be over unless you are under the things God wants you to be under. You can only walk in authority over the areas God has entrusted to you if you are living under the full authority of Jesus Christ. If you live under the authority of Jesus and under the control of the Spirit, your expression of authority will always manifest the life of God.

What does it mean to walk under authority?

How did Jesus walk under authority?

What does it look like to live under the authority of Jesus daily?

What happens when a man tries to walk in authority without living under authority?

Being Christians means our wills are completely submissive to the will of God. How is that manifested in your life? How are you daily submitting to God's will?

PERSONAL STUDY 5

Walking in Authority

Read Ephesians 2:4-6.

The more you walk under authority, the more you will be able to walk in authority. This is true because as you walk in authority, you will be sensitive to the call of Jesus. You will no longer be passive but aggressive in your obedience to Jesus. But what does this look like? Walking in authority is most often manifested in three ways.

First, we walk in our authority by standing. More specifically, we do this by aggressively taking our stand against the enemy. Because of our union with Christ, we are not only united with Jesus in His death, burial, and resurrection, we are also united with Him in his ascension (Ephesians 2:4-6). This means, we have been given authority to take our stand against sin and Satan (Ephesians 6:10-11; 1 Peter 5:8-9; James 4:7).

We do not passively sit by while the enemy assaults us. We stand against the enemy by the power of the Spirit and the truth of His Word. We use our God-given weapons to take our stand against all that is opposed to Christ (2 Corinthians 10:4).

Second, we walk in authority by leading. Revisit our study on assignments and the areas where God has called you to lead. If God has given you leadership, He expects you to walk under and in His authority. Anything less is a failure to be faithful to His calling.

When a man fails to lead in his assignments, he harms those under his charge, and he rebels against the One who gave those responsibilities. You are called to walk in your God-given authority, as God has called you, in every area God has assigned to you.

Finally, we walk in authority by protecting. We must not fail as Adam did to protect those we are responsible for (Genesis 3:1-6). We are called to protect our wives, children, churches, and communities. We protect them against the subtle attacks of the enemy, the demonic pull of the world, and the drifting of our culture. There is a lion on the loose, and we must act like it.

Why can a man walk in authority more faithfully when he is walking under authority?

How do walking in authority and walking under authority affect and complement each other?

What does it mean to walk in authority by standing? How can you apply that?

What does it mean to walk in authority by leading? How can you apply that?

What does it mean to walk in authority by protecting? How can you apply that?

The Titus Ten

Character

Group Study

START

Welcome to week 6 of The Titus Ten.
Use this page to get the conversation going.

Last week, we talked about the importance of being a man who stewards his authority. To do this well, we must also be men of character.

What was the most helpful idea you learned or wrestled with last week?

What are some ways men develop godly character?

Being a manly man is not about possessing certain so-called manly skills. Being a manly man is ultimately about possessing a certain manly character. The Bible teaches that certain qualities are associated with manliness. There is such a thing as a manly man. There always has been.

When it comes to calling men into true manhood, we can be tempted to focus on the externals. Books and conferences for men tend to tell us that we must tap into our true inner outdoorsman to discover manhood. But a call to outward actions does not cultivate a man. Inward character makes a man. Therefore, the call to be a man is a call to apply great diligence to the cultivation of Christian character (Titus 1:10-16).

Our goal is not just to be good men. Our goal is to be godly men. Our goal is to manifest the character of Jesus Christ. You must cultivate your inner man, because your inner man is the man you really are.

WATCH

Use this page to take notes as you watch video session 6.

To access the teaching sessions,
use the instructions in the back
of your Bible study book.

DISCUSS

Use this page to facilitate the group discussion.

Read 1 Corinthians 16:13 together.

How does our culture tend to define a "manly man"?

The apostle Paul ended his letter to the church in Corinth by saying, "Be watchful, stand firm in the faith, act like men, be strong" (1 Corinthians 16:13). The phrase "act like men" could also be translated as "be courageous." Although this could be a call for every man and woman in the church to be courageous, this word in the original Greek meant "to behave like a man." Paul used this phrase because he knew there were certain qualities, both culturally and biblically, that were manly.

How does the world's definition of a "manly man" differ from the biblical definition?

Centuries before Paul, David expressed the same idea in the speech he gave in his dying days to his son Solomon. David began his final words with, "I am about to go the way of the earth. Be strong, and show yourself a man" (1 Kings 2:2). David was calling his son Solomon to act in a distinctly manly way. He was calling him to be a man's man.

God calls every male to "act like a man." But this is not a call to embrace some kind of manly bravado or to learn certain manly skills. It does not refer to outward manly actions as much as it refers to an inward manly character.

When it comes to manhood, why do we tend to focus on external activities more than internal character?

Read Titus 1:5-9. How did Paul describe the men who should lead the church? What do you notice about their character? ?

What do you think are the primary character qualities that make a man?

What men in your life embody these characteristics?

What masculine characteristics can you identify in the life and ministry of Jesus?

We must cultivate godly character because everything else flows from it. The goal of this study is not just to be a good man but to be a godly man. Jesus Christ is the most perfectly masculine man who has ever lived. To be a manly man is to be like Jesus. We define manly character by how closely it aligns with Jesus.

What are some ways we can spur one another on to develop our character?

End your time together by praying for one another. Remind the group to complete the five days of personal study prior to the next group meeting.

We Must Cultivate Character

Read 2 Peter 1:3-11.

Character is something that must be cultivated. No one becomes a man of character by accident. We must apply great effort to become the men God has called us to be. Specifically, we are to become men who manifest the character God expects.

God wants you to work hard to cultivate godly virtues. And since certain virtues are more distinctly manly, every man who chooses to follow Jesus must choose to work hard at cultivating these virtues. We must, as 2 Peter 1:5 said, "make every effort."

For some reason, people tend to view Christian growth unlike any other area of growth. A student does not just "let go and let God" if he wants to do well on an exam—he must study. A golfer does not get better by resting in his desire to be better—he practices. An entrepreneur does not succeed by sitting in his office dreaming of success—he works. But for some reason, we often think growth in Christlikeness happens passively!

The Bible continually calls us to give our greatest effort to what is of greatest importance—our relationship with Jesus Christ. In Philippians 2:12–13, Paul said it this way: "Therefore, my beloved, as you have always obeyed, so now, not only as in my presence but much more in my absence, work out your own salvation with fear and trembling, for it is God who works in you, both to will and to work for his good pleasure." In other words, believers must continue to work *out* what God continues to work *in*. We cannot "work in" our salvation; only God can do that. But we must "work out" our salvation by applying great diligence.

Our spiritual life is like any other area of our life—growth demands effort. Christian character does not appear out of nowhere or by chance; it is cultivated.

What kind of effort did Peter say we should apply to cultivating Christian character in 2 Peter 1:5-8?

What did Peter say is the benefit of cultivating character?

We cannot work "in" our salvation—only God can do that. But according to Philippians 2:12-13, we must work "out" our salvation. What kind of effort does that require?

What are some specific character qualities you would like to grow in or feel that you need to grow in?

What effort are you currently making to develop those qualities? How can you begin to make more effort in the cultivation of those qualities?

The Qualities That Make a Man

Read Titus 1:10-16.

Paul left Titus in Crete because the church was a mess. Paul instructed Titus to bring order back to the church. But what was the first thing that needed to be done to establish order in the church? Paul told Titus that his first priority was to "appoint elders in every town" (v. 5). The greatest need in that highly dysfunctional church was godly men.

This church had men, but not the right kind. It was filled with "empty talkers and deceivers" (v. 10), "lazy gluttons" (v. 12), and men who were "detestable, disobedient, unfit for any good work" (v. 16). And Paul told Titus exactly what kind of men he should look for.

One thing interesting about Paul's description of godly men is that he did not tell Titus to look primarily for intelligence, education, talent, or popularity. Paul told Titus to look for men of strong character (vv. 5-9). Paul told Timothy the same thing, and gave him a very similar list (1 Timothy 3:1-7). What makes this list so significant is it gives us a clear paradigm of the kind of men we all should aspire to be, even if we don't aspire to be pastors. What Paul was saying to both Timothy and Titus was, "Here is what a godly man looks like. Go find men like this and give them leadership."

These two lists say to us, "Here is the kind of man God is looking for. This is what it means to be a man of character." Although 1 Timothy and Titus lay out twenty character qualities of a man of God, and each one deserves our prayerful attention and active cultivation, these qualities can be summarized in three broad categories: blamelessness, self-control, and courage. We will look at each of these over the next three days.

What affect can bad men have on a church? What affect can godly men have on a church?

How have you seen men with a lack of character destroy a church, a family, or a nation?

Why does character matter so much in a man's life?

As you read the list of qualifications for an elder, what qualities stood out the most? Why?

Why does character matter more than skill?

Being Blameless

Read 1 Timothy 3:2-12.

There is one overarching quality every man must cultivate. All other qualities flow from this one. It is so significant, that in Paul's list of qualifications for Titus, he mentioned it twice. It is the quality of blamelessness.

To be blameless means to be a man of unquestionable integrity. It means you are the man in private that you appear to be in public. There are two primary areas in which we must seek to be blameless: at home and in the community.

Without any hesitation, Paul moved from the quality of blamelessness to a man's life at home. The probing question becomes, "Could your family share things about your life that would damage your reputation and disqualify you from leadership?"

Those closest to you are going to see the best and worst in you. Those closest to you will see your sin the most. They see you when you are the most tired, grumpy, frustrated, and angry. No man is without fault at home. So, the issue is not that you aren't perfect. The issue is how you respond when you are at fault at home.

Someone once said that being blameless at home is "righting your wrongs." You will do wrong over and over again. But the question is, do you make it right? Those closest to you need to see you repent, weep over your sin, and say you are sorry.

Your blamelessness is also manifested in the community. Paul said that a man must not be "open to the charge of debauchery or insubordination" (Titus 1:6). This asks the question, "Is there anyone out there with incriminating evidence against you?"

Are there people at work, in your neighborhood, on the ball field, or on the golf course who could tell stories that would surprise others? Are there any women who could bring judgment on you by the way you have looked at or talked to her?

The starting place for cultivating manly character is the pursuit of blamelessness. It is striving, by the power of the gospel of Jesus Christ, to live a life of integrity.

What does it mean to be blameless?

What are the two primary areas in which you need to be blameless?
Why do these two areas matter the most?

Being blameless does not mean being without fault. No one is without fault.
Rather, it is acknowledging your faults and repenting of them. In what ways
do you need to do that right now?

What areas of your life would keep you from being blameless?

Are there people in the community that could bring accusation against you?
If so, in what specific areas could they do that?

Self-Control

Read Titus 2:1-10.

After laying the foundation of blamelessness, Paul gave a list of eleven qualities—five negatives and six positives. Yet every one of them demand one quality that is mentioned twice in Titus 1:8: "self-controlled" and "disciplined." In other words, you will never be a man of strong character unless you are first a man of strong self-discipline.

Look back at the five negative qualities Paul said destroy a man's character in Titus 1:7-8. They are arrogant, quick-tempered, drunkard, violent, and greedy for gain. Although each one of those deserves careful consideration, the over-arching issue is the lack of self-control.

In chapter 2, as Titus received specific instruction for each group in the church, he was commanded to teach the older men and older women to have self-control. But the most interesting mention of self-control is in Titus 2:6. After giving a series of instructions to older men and older women, Paul only gives one admonition to young men. He says, "Likewise, urge the younger men to be self-controlled." Is there anything a young man needs to learn more than self-control?

Here is the thing about self-control: If you don't learn it when you are a young man, you end up developing habits that affect you when you are old. Those areas in which you lack self-control don't go away! They don't get better, they get bigger.

Self-control in one area always leads to greater self-control in other area, and a lack of self-control in one area often leads to lack of self-control in other areas. Cultivating self-control begins with the smaller areas of life. It begins with a disciplined time with the Lord every day. Gain control of your eating, commit to regular exercise, start coming home from work on time, and commit to consistent and personal time with your children. You cultivate discipline in the small areas of your life to become a disciplined, self-controlled person overall.

There will be no growth in any area of Christian character without the slow and steady cultivation of self-control.

How often was self-control mentioned in our reading for the day? Why do you think that one issue receives so much attention?

Why does every character deficiency go back to a lack of self-control? How do you see that manifested in your life?

Why do you think self-control is the only thing mentioned for young men to cultivate?

How does learning self-control as a young man affect you as an older man?

In what specific areas do you need to display more self-control?

Courage

Read Joshua 1:6-9.

Many organizations, churches, families, and countries have systemic problems that are all rooted in the lack of courage among the men. If a man is not willing to do hard things, make hard decisions, and suffer for what is right, everyone around him suffers. This is true in an organization, a church, a home, and a nation.

Men are called to have courage. The courage to stand. The courage to speak. The courage to act. God's call on your life demands courage, and one of the greatest tactics of the enemy is to get you to be passive. The enemy wants to trade a courageous heart with a quiet and cowardly heart. We must fight our tendency toward cowardice and passivity by cultivating a courageous heart.

True courage is not just the strength to do difficult things; it is the strength to do the right thing. True courage is the willingness to do the godly thing. True courage does not just take a stand; it takes a stand for godliness.

Psalm 31:24 says, "Be strong, and let your heart take courage, all you who wait for the Lord!" Our courage flows from confidence in the Lord. As our confidence in God increases, so does our courage. When godly men act with courage, it is because they are deeply rooted in the confidence of God.

As you walk with the Lord, you will not only grow in courage; you will grow in your ability to discern when that courage is needed. You will develop the depth of character that is needed to know what is right and do it, no matter the cost. As your faith in God grows, so will your confidence.

Every assignment in your life demands courage, because every assignment in your life is hard. You will never use your plow and sword without courage. You will never live out your true identity or walk in authority without courage. Courage is not an option; it is a necessity. A manly man is a courageous man.

How have you seen a lack of courage among men destroy a church, a family, or a community?

Why it is often challenging to be courageous?

How does our confidence in God affect our courage?

If courage flows from confidence in God, what would be most important in cultivating more courage?

Is there any area in your life where others are suffering because of your lack of courage? If so, what action do you need to take?

The Titus Ten

Week 7

Doctrine

Group Study

START

Thus far in the study, we have tackled crucial questions of what godly men are like. This week, we will examine what godly men believe.

What challenged or encouraged you from last week's personal study?

How important is it for you to have firm convictions about what you believe?

The book of Titus gives us a vision for men that is very different than the one we often see today. Titus gives us a vision of men who are deeply rooted in the Word of God and apply great effort in seeking knowledge of God. Godly men understand that the most important area of our lives deserves the greatest effort of our lives.

To be the men God has called us to be, we must be deeply immersed in God's Word.

WATCH

Use this page to take notes as you watch video session 7.

To access the teaching sessions,
use the instructions in the back
of your Bible study book.

DISCUSS

Use this page to facilitate the group discussion.

Although this vision for men can be seen throughout the book of Titus, it is summarized in one primary verse.

Read Titus 1:9 together. How would you summarize this verse in your own words?

It seems rare to find men in the church who apply themselves to diligent study of the Word. Why do you think that is?

What is the hindrance to your deep study of God's Word?

Even though this verse addresses those aspiring to the office of an elder/pastor, it is also a picture of God's desire for every man. Every man has been called to grow in the grace and knowledge of Jesus Christ. Being godly men is not just about who we are, it is also about what we know. Paul made it clear he wants every man in the church to be sound in the faith (Titus 1:13). Titus gave a fresh vision of what a godly man looks like — a vision of men deeply rooted in sound doctrine.

Sometimes people seem to believe sound doctrine and aggressive action oppose each other, as if some men study and some men work. But this is not what Scripture teaches. The book of Titus consistently combines sound doctrine and fruitful action (Titus 1:1; 1:9; 1:13; 2:1-2; 2:7-8; 3:8). There is a clear connection between thinking right and doing right. Those who know God are better equipped to serve God.

Why does right knowledge of God lead to more fruitful action for God?

Why is a deep knowledge of God and His Word so important for men?

There is no virtue in ignorance. We should never settle for having a mind that is not filled with what is most important. If God is of greatest value, He deserves our greatest thought.

Think back to your domains. How would you be further equipped to take dominion in those areas of life if you knew the Word of God better?

What are some ways we can help one another develop in these areas?

End your time together by praying for one another. Remind the group to complete the five days of personal study prior to the next group meeting.

Deeply Rooted

Read Psalm 1.

Psalm 1 is one of the most important passages of Scripture for every man of God to memorize and meditate on. It paints a picture of a deeply rooted tree bearing fruit and not withering. It is a vision of what every man should aspire to be.

The idea of being "rooted" like an old oak tree is essential in the pursuit of godliness. One of Paul's most frequent exhortations was to "stand firm in the faith." First Corinthians 16:13 says, "Be watchful, stand firm in the faith, act like men, be strong." Paul gave this call in almost every letter he wrote. It is impossible to stand firm if you are not deeply rooted.

How do we become deeply rooted? According to Psalm 1, it is by delighting in the law of the Lord and meditating on it day and night. We are deeply rooted through years of consistent meditation, memorization, reading, and study of God's Word. A man who is unwilling to dedicate himself to consistent time in the Word of God will never be a godly man.

Every man should want to be "like a tree, planted by streams of water, that yields its fruit in season, and its leaf does not wither? In all that he does, he prospers" (v. 3). What could be better than that? What a joy to know you lived in a way that produced fruit and prospered in every area.

That life is not just possible, it is promised. But only to those who will take God's Word seriously. It is promised to those who don't just read the Word but meditate on it and store it deep in our hearts. We should not only be captured by the vision of what we can be but also motivated to apply the effort it takes to become that man. We pursue living as deeply rooted trees by pursuing the knowledge of God through His Word.

What encourages and motivates you as you read Psalm 1?

What does a man need to become the man described in Psalm 1?

What must a man avoid to be the man described in Psalm 1?

What practical things do you need to do to become that man?

How would those around you benefit from you being a deeply rooted man?

Sound Doctrine

Read Titus 1:10-16.

When Paul told Titus to look for men who "hold firm to the trustworthy word, so that he may be able to instruct in sound doctrine and also to rebuke those who contradict it" (Titus 1:9), he was telling Titus to look for men who were deeply rooted in sound doctrine. Sound doctrine makes up the roots, but what exactly is sound doctrine?

When Paul wrote about doctrine, he was referring to the truth God has revealed about Himself. Where "trustworthy word" might refer to God's revelation in His Word, "doctrine" would refer to the specific truths contained in the Word. For example, if you were to buy a book on basic Bible doctrines, you would find topics such as the Bible, God, mankind, salvation, and the church. These chapters would be a summary of what the Bible as a whole says about those specific topics. Doctrine is truth.

The word *sound* means healthy. To have *sound doctrine* means you have doctrine that leads to life—doctrine that heals, nurtures, and feeds. The vision for manhood here is that every man seeks not only to read and understand the Bible but to have a good working knowledge of the major truths of God's Word. This is the kind of knowledge that heals, nurtures, and feeds those under a man's care. This is part of taking dominion. Being rooted in sound doctrine is essential to fulfilling your role as a man.

This admonition is a call to take seriously that which is most serious—namely, God and the truth about Him. This is a call to seek for Him like silver and search for Him like a hidden treasure (Proverbs 2:4). This is a call to not settle for a surface understanding of God but seek to know the doctrine that leads to godliness.

Titus 1:10-16 shows the damaging effects of men who do not have sound doctrine? What were the effects on the church as Paul saw it?

How have you seen a lack of sound doctrine affect families and churches?

Why is sound doctrine essential to a healthy church and a healthy family?

How does doctrine lead to godliness?

Does your study of doctrine reflect the pursuit described in Proverbs 2:4? If not, why not and what can you do to change that?

Why You Need Doctrine, Part 1

Read Titus 2:11-15.

The word *doctrine* does not seem to excite many men. But when we talk about doctrine, we are talking about knowing God. We are talking about being a sound, solid, rooted man who not only knows the truths of God but can also teach them to others. There are four primary reasons you need doctrine.

You need doctrine to understand the gospel. There is nothing more important than this—not just for yourself but all those God has placed under your influence. The gospel is both incredibly simple and profoundly deep. That is clear from our reading in Titus 2.

This message is simple. God sent His Son into this world to save sinners. But there is so much beauty, glory, and life-forming truth in this summary of the gospel: seeing Jesus as the appearing of God's grace; understanding how the gospel not only saves us but also trains us; knowing the hope that awaits us when Jesus returns; feeling the weight, cost, and joy of redemption; realizing God is gathering for Himself a distinct people who manifest His glory through their good works. These are incredible truths!

Seek to understand the gospel in its fullness. The gospel does not just save us; the gospel changes us, forms us, empowers us, and infuses us with hope for today. You need to swim in it and let it constantly change you. That is what doctrine is for.

You also need doctrine to understand the Bible. Most people do not know the basic storyline of the Bible. They do not see the Bible as one united story of God's plan to save His people by the sacrifice of His Son. If you do not understand the basic storyline of the Bible, you will misunderstand, misinterpret, and often be confused by most of the Bible.

Doctrine matters because the Bible matters. Every man must understand the Word of God so He might apply it to his own life and teach it to others. This is not possible without the pursuit of doctrine.

What do we mean when we use the word *doctrine?*

Why does doctrine matter so much?

Can you clearly articulate the message of the gospel? Take time now to do so.

How does the gospel not only change our eternity, but also our present reality?
In other words, why does it matter practically if you understand the gospel well?

Why it is so important to understand the basic story of the Bible?
Do you understand that story?

Why You Need Doctrine, Part 2

Read Deuteronomy 6:1-9.

You not only need doctrine to understand the gospel and understand God's Word, you need doctrine to be able to teach the Word. Although God has not called every man to be a pastor, he has called every man, in some form or fashion, to teach the Word.

You teach the Word when you share the gospel with an unbeliever. You teach the Word when you get into a discussion about creation, sexuality, ethics, or marriage. You teach the Word when a coworker, classmate, or friend asks you any question about God. You teach the Word when you lead your family in devotions. This is certainly true for fathers. The primary place for theological instruction is in the home (Deuteronomy 6). This means every father must know how to teach the Word.

You learn to understand and teach the Word as you choose to dive a little deeper into the basic truths of the Word—first for the sake of your own relationship with the Lord, and then for the sake of everyone around you, especially those under your authority.

Finally, you need doctrine so you can guard the truth. Our faith is constantly under attack. Every day the truth is challenged. But this doesn't just come in the obvious ways. Satan is like a prowling lion, looking to devour believers (1 Peter 5:8). We know he's the father of lies (John 8:44). But we should also remember that he comes disguised as an angel of light (2 Corinthians 11:14). Satan is too crafty to come at us only through a full-frontal attack; like he did with Eve, he comes with subtlety, deception, and cleverness (Genesis 3:1-6).

As much as we need to know the basic doctrines of Scripture, today, being able to communicate the basic truths is not really enough. We need to know how to engage in conversations about sexual ethics, the sanctity of marriage and human life, and discerning truth from lies. Every man must seek to be a protector of the truth.

In what ways, formally or informally, are you responsible to communicate God's Word?

Why is the knowledge of doctrine important in sharing your faith and leading your family?

In today's culture, why is it not sufficient for Christian men to be uninformed on doctrine? Why is doctrine so important in the days in which we live?

In what ways do you see the lack of doctrine affecting the church as a whole?

How is your knowledge of God essential for protecting and guarding the faith?

Becoming Sound in Doctrine

Read Proverbs 3:13-18.

The Spirit-filled study of doctrine always leads men to be stronger, more active, and more effective in the work of the Lord. It leads men to be more faithful in every one of their God-given assignments. So how do you grow in doctrine?

It begins with desire. You will never pursue something you do not desire. As Proverbs 3:13-18 teaches, nothing we desire compares in value to the knowledge of God. Some of you already feel that desire. If so, praise the Lord. If you do not, pray for it. Desire comes from God. God will give you this desire if you ask for it and seek it. Ask God to give you a passion and longing for truth.

Desire must then lead to discipline. We discipline ourselves for godliness. There is no growth in any area of life without discipline. Desiring to lose weight has never made anyone skinny. That desire must lead to discipline. So it is with our desire for truth. The desire must manifest itself in a life that makes truth a priority (1 Timothy 4:7–8).

There are many helpful resources for growing in doctrine: using a good study Bible, trying to better understand one specific book of the Bible at a time, using commentaries, reading a book on the storyline of the Bible, studying a confession of faith, or even getting a book on basic Bible doctrines.

All of these things can help, but without question, the most important thing is a commitment to regular Bible reading. Don't run to theology books first. Run to the Bible. No area of our life will grow unless we are committed to regular time in God's Word. Start with a chapter a day, but don't stop there. Consume the Word. Treat it like the treasure it is. Go after it.

How would growth in doctrine help you in every area of your God-given assignments?

Do you have a desire for more knowledge of God? If so, how are you pursing that? If not, how will you seek that desire?

Desire must be followed by discipline. How can you better discipline yourself to grow in doctrine?

Are you regularly and consistently reading your Bible? If not, what hinders you from doing so?

In addition to regularly Bible reading, what resources will you begin to use or what action will you take to grow in doctrine?

The Titus Ten

Mission

Group Study

START

Welcome to week 8 of **The Titus Ten.**
Use this page to get the conversation going.

Last week, we talked about cultivating deeply held beliefs based on the Word of God. This week, we will talk about how our beliefs lead us to action.

Share one key insight you gained from last week's study.

How do our beliefs inform our actions?

You were created for a mission. It's in your DNA. Every man has something in him that wants to attempt great things, accomplish great things, and be a part of great things. There is, in the heart of every man, even if he has never identified it, a desire to be a part of something greater than himself.

When men do not have a compelling mission, they respond in different ways. Some settle for a life of mediocrity and the mundane, assuming they just need to bury their boyish dreams and ambitions. Others become desperately bored and, in an attempt to find something more exciting in life, make foolish decisions. Others will be driven by a constant sense of dissatisfaction, causing them to repeatedly leave what they have in a desperate search for something better—something more exciting.

Men were created for a mission. In the absence of one they will chase other things. However, God has given each of us a mission to build His kingdom.

WATCH

Use this page to take notes as you watch video session 8.

To access the teaching sessions,
use the instructions in the back
of your Bible study book.

DISCUSS

Use this page to facilitate the group discussion.

Men long for a fight. Men want to be a part of a battle. Men want to stand for justice and make wrong things right—to participate in something bigger than themselves. Men are naturally allergic to boredom. And this desire for a mission has led mankind to do some incredible things.

This is not just anecdotal. Men were created for a mission. Without some grand, life-consuming mission, you will never feel as if your life matters.

Do you sense that you were created for a mission? What are some ways you feel that in your life?

Most men suppress their desire for a compelling mission? Why do you think men do that? Where do you sense you have done that?

When men do not have a mission, they respond in different ways. How do you see men responding in negative ways because of their lack of mission?

How have you seen men destroy their lives because they were searching for something to fulfill the lack of mission?

Why are men without a mission dangerous?

In simplistic terms, isn't this the source of most midlife crises? There is a stage in a man's life when he wakes up and thinks, *Is this it? Is this as good as it's going to get? Wasn't life supposed to be more exciting than this?* Those questions lead men into feelings of boredom, emptiness, and rebellion. So, without any greater mission, they turn back into rebellious teenagers and make damaging decisions.

Read Matthew 28:18-20 and Luke 9:1-6.

Describe the mission that Jesus sends each of us on in your own words.
How are you taking part in His mission for your life?

Men without a mission are dangerous to themselves and everyone around them. Men must have a mission. If this desire for a mission is not properly discovered, cultivated, and empowered, the results can be catastrophic. This is why every man must understand his role in the mission of God.

God's design is not just to save you. God's design is to send you. God's design is to do something in you and then do something through you. Men were created to receive from God and to take what they're received from God into the world for His purposes and His glory. We need to know and declare the gospel to a lost and broken culture. Participating in the mission of God will bring us the purpose our otherwise aimless hearts long for.

End your time together by praying for one another. Remind the group to complete the five days of personal study prior to the next group meeting.

The Mission of God

Read Psalm 96.

You were created for a mission because you were created in the image of a missionary God. God has always had a mission. God did not create mankind and then realize they would be bored without something to do. God created mankind to fulfill His mission.

We see the mission of God in the garden of Eden before sin even entered the picture. Eden was the place of God's presence. Eden was the temple of God. Adam and Eve found their complete fulfillment in Eden because God was there, walking among them (Genesis 3:8). True life is always found in the presence of God. You exist for His presence and only discover life in His presence. This is a picture of life as it was meant to be.

The presence of God in the garden is symbolized by the river flowing out of Eden. Genesis 2:10 says, "A river flowed out of Eden to water the garden, and there it divided and became four rivers." The river flowing out of Eden symbolizes the very presence of God giving life to everything in Eden. But there was more than one river in the garden.

The river flowing out of the garden divided into four different rivers. If the river flowing into the garden represents the presence of God bringing life to Eden, the four rivers flowing out of the garden represent the presence of God flowing outward, bringing life to all nations.

And this is the heart of God. God has created all of mankind to be truly satisfied only in His presence. Because we were created for God, and will only find satisfaction in God, God desires to spread His presence to the ends of the earth.

God's mission has always been that all people know Him and enjoy His presence for eternity. Therefore, the greatest demonstration of God's love is to call all people to come into His presence through Jesus Christ and worship Him. This is the mission you were created for.

What does Psalm 96 tell us about the heart and mission of God?

What do we learn about God's mission from the garden of Eden?

What does the river flowing into the garden symbolize and what do the rivers flowing out of the garden symbolize? What does that teach us about God's heart and mission?

Why is God's presence a central part of God's mission?

Describe the mission of God in your own words.

The Mission of Man

Read Titus 3:8-11.

The book of Titus shows us an important transition that every man must make. Titus 1 focuses on a man and the church. Titus 2 focuses on a man and the family. But Titus 3 moves outside the church and the home into the world. A man must not only be faithful in his church and in his home, he must be a faithful witness to the world. Every man must embrace the mission of God.

When Jesus called His disciples, He did so with two words: "Follow me" (Luke 5:27). It was a call both to trust and follow Jesus. The disciples had no idea of the adventure that awaited them when they accepted that invitation. In the following days, weeks, months, and years, they would see Jesus heal the sick, calm storms, cast out demons, raise the dead, preach to multitudes, and publicly expose the religious Pharisees of the day. If any man thinks following Jesus is boring and unengaging, it is because he is not following Jesus.

When we come to the Great Commission passages (Matthew 28:18–20; Mark 16:15; Luke 24:44–49; John 20:21; Acts 1:8), we sense the same kind of excitement. Although there is much to say about each of these passages, essentially Jesus was looking at His disciples and saying, "Go do for others what I did for you." The simplicity of the Commission is summarized in Jesus's words in John 20:21, when He said, "As the Father has sent me, even so I am sending you."

God is calling you to trust and follow Jesus, and as you discover what this means in your life, you reproduce that. The mission of man is to lead people to trust and follow Jesus. This is what Jesus did, and this is, in the simplest terms, what Jesus is calling us to do. We begin by calling people to trust and follow Jesus through the proclamation of the gospel and then continue to call them to trust and follow Jesus through the ongoing teaching of God's Word.

What important transition in the book of Titus must every man make?

Why is that transition so difficult for many men? In other words, why are so many men faithful at home and at church but not faithful witnesses for Jesus?

What are the biggest hindrances that keep you from sharing the gospel?

Summarize your understanding of the mission of God from the Great Commission passages.

In what ways can you more effectively engage with God in His mission?

Declaring and Displaying

Read Titus 3:1-7.

If our model for mission is found in Jesus, then our mission must include both declaring and displaying the gospel. When Jesus preached, "The kingdom of God is at hand" (Mark 1:15), He went on both to declare and display the kingdom. Everywhere He went He preached the gospel of the kingdom and displayed the kingdom through His work.

The way we engage with God in His mission is still the same. We join God in His mission by declaring and displaying the gospel of the kingdom. The gospel must be declared. We must embrace our responsibility to share verbally the good news of Jesus Christ.

Verbally sharing the gospel is a challenge for many of us. It might be the fear of man, a sense of inadequacy, insecurity, or spiritual warfare. But we must pray that God would deliver us from those things and make us bold enough to openly talk about Jesus.

But the gospel must not only be declared; it must also be displayed. Titus 3:1-2 gives us a reminder that our outward actions have a massive impact on the fulfillment of our mission. Our mission is not just to speak well; our mission is to live well. We are all called to "show perfect courtesy toward all people" (v. 2).

Imagine the power and influence of your life if you just took that one phrase seriously. Imagine the impact you would make if your life was marked by "perfect courtesy." You would be displaying the gospel in a way most people have never seen.

God did not just save you so you would attend church and act nice when you get there. God saved you to transform you. And He intended for that inner transformation to be manifested in your outward actions. He saved you so that every moment of your life would have significance, because every moment of your life is a part of His mission.

Our model for missions must include two elements. What are they?

Why are both of these essential for being an effective witness?

Which one of these do you find the most challenging personally? Why?

When it was the last time you verbally shared the gospel? What hinders you from doing so? How could you be more faithful in this area?

Are there any areas of your life in which you are not displaying the gospel? Are there any places in which you need to be more careful to display the gospel? Explain.

Every Neighbor, Every Nation

Read Psalm 67.

If we are going to embrace the mission of God and fulfill the desire God has placed in our hearts for mission, we must also embrace the call to make sure every neighbor and every nation hears the gospel. Our mission field includes those around us and those who live in the hardest to reach places on earth.

Our missionary assignment begins with our neighbors. It must. We must see those in our family, workplace, school, neighborhood, and community as those God has called us to reach and think carefully and strategically about how to reach them. But our vision is not just reaching every neighbor; it is reaching every nation. Our vision must include every nation because God's mission includes every nation (Psalm 67).

At the time of writing this Bible study, there are around seven thousand unreached people groups in the world. A people group is considered "unreached" means they don't have access to the gospel, that Jesus isn't well known in the area, or that the church population there doesn't have the means to share about Jesus without help from other Christians. About three billion people in those groups are considered unreached.[3]

Of those unreached people groups, there are three thousand who are considered unengaged, unreached people groups. These groups have no Christian presence and have no known church planting activity underway. It is estimated that more than 157,000 people die every day without any access to the gospel.[4]

Right now, God is calling you to step into His mission by declaring and displaying the gospel to those around you. And as you step out in faith and engage in His mission to your neighbors, He will cultivate in you an increasing passion to see more people come to Christ. You will not only long to see your neighbors come to Christ, but you will also begin to feel a burden for the nations. We are to make this the greatest aim of our life until every neighbor and every nation hears the glorious news of Jesus Christ.

Who around you needs to hear the gospel? Make a list of those people and begin to pray regularly for them.

How could you more faithfully engage those around you with the gospel?

Are you burdened by the lost around you and the lost around the world? If not, why do you think that is? Begin praying for a burden for the lost.

How can you more faithfully pray for the unreached peoples around the world? What practical steps can you take to be more mindful of the lost nations?

Not everyone can go to the ends of the earth to take the gospel to the unreached, but everyone must be involved. In what ways can you get involved?

PERSONAL STUDY 5

Fuel the Fire

Read Romans 10:1-4.

When God begins to work in our hearts and give us a desire to see people saved, it is like a fire that rages in us. You may have felt that fire at some point in your life. Some feel it when a missionary comes to speak, when they attend a missions conference, or when they go on a mission trip. But anyone who has experienced the fire for missions has also felt how easy it is for that fire to go out.

Most men have very little, if any, fire for seeing lost people come to Christ. Others once had a fire that is nothing but dying embers. The reality is, we all tend to be self-centered and consumed with our little worlds, and we must fight to keep a passion for the lost. The question is, how can we keep a fire in our hearts for the lost?

First, we must pray and ask God for a burden and a passion for His mission. God must give us a deep longing for people to come to Christ.

Then, we must fuel the fire through daily pursuit of the presence of God. A man will never be passionate about spreading the presence of God unless he is passionate about experiencing the presence of God. Where there is no passion flowing in, there will never be passion flowing out.

We must also faithfully and consistently fuel the fire in practical ways. When we have lost people in our home, engage in conversations and make friends with the lost, and simply spend more time with those who don't know Christ, it increases our burden. When we read missionary biographies, learn more about unreached peoples, and go on short term mission trips, it keeps the fire burning.

The mission of God is the noblest, most adventurous, and compelling cause in all of the world. It is what you have been created for. It is the great calling of your life. And it begins now. It begins where you are. It begins with declaring and displaying the gospel to your neighbor. And it does not end until the last unreached people group hears the glorious message of Jesus Christ and people from every nation, tribe, and nation stand before the throne giving their worship to Him (Revelation 7:9).

Has there been a time in your life when you had more passion for the lost than you do now? What changed?

How can you commit to pray regularly for God to give you this passion?

What practical ways can you fuel a passion for the lost in your life? Would you consider pursuing a short term mission trip?

Who are some specific lost people you need to spend more time with?

How can you make sure that you are keeping the mission of God before you and not losing sight of it?

Zeal

Group Study

START

Welcome to week 9 of The Titus Ten.
Use this page to get the conversation going.

Last week, we dove into the mission that God has given every man. On our second to last week, we're going to be talking about zeal.

What is one way you're taking what you're learning in the this study and applying it to your life?

What is something you would say that you're zealous for?

The Titus Ten contains a lot of information. It is intended to be foundational. It is deeply rooted in truth and is meant to be a theological framework for your life. But the real prayer of participating in this Bible study is that we would develop into men like Jesus, who have a zeal for God. God's design, and the great need of this generation, is for men to have godly zeal.

WATCH

Use this page to take notes as you watch video session 9.

To access the teaching sessions,
use the instructions in the back
of your Bible study book.

DISCUSS

Use this page to facilitate the group discussion.

Read the account of Jesus overturning the tables in John 2:13-17. Why is this moment so surprising? What do we see about Jesus that we don't expect?

What do you think made Jesus respond that way? Why were His actions so dramatic?

Jesus did not sin in doing this, so why do you think this was not only justified but also good and right?

When we read the Gospels, we expect Jesus to do miracles. We expect Him to preach and demonstrate His power and authority. When we come to the end of the story, we even expect His death, burial, and resurrection. Those moments do not surprise us.

What we don't expect is for Jesus to take the time to carefully handcraft a whip, make His way to the temple, and use the whip to drive people out. We don't expect Him to pour out the coins of the money changers, overturn tables (John 2:15), and declare, "Do not make my father's house a house of trade" (John 2:16). And we really don't expect him to do it twice (John 2:16; Matthew 21.12-17).

If we are shocked by just reading it, it's hard to image how shocked the disciples were to actually be there. John tells us that as the disciples tried to process this moment, they remembered what David said: "Zeal for your house has consumed me" (Psalm 69:9). Through the revelation of the Holy Spirit, the disciples understood this psalm to be speaking of Jesus. What they were seeing in Jesus could be summarized in one word: *zeal*.

Read Titus 2:14. God wants zealous people. What do you think that means? What would it look like to be "zealous for good works"?

In Titus 2, after giving specific instruction to the people of the church, Paul told Titus to train up believers to not only believe and live the gospel, but train people to be zealous for good works (Titus 2:11-14).

Do you know any men that have a zeal for God? How does that manifest itself? Why do you think we see so little of that zeal?

God has always been assembling a people for His own possession (Exodus 19:5; Ezekiel 37:23). His plan has always been to choose, rescue, redeem, and use a people to manifest His glory. And His intention has always been that these people, whom He has called by His name and chosen for His glory, would be zealous for good works. God wants zealous people.

Is there something or someone other than God that you are giving your zeal? What adjustments might you need to make? How can we help one another pursue God with a heart of gratitude for the grace that He's given us?

End your time together by praying for one another. Remind the group to complete the five days of personal study prior to the next group meeting.

The Three Parts of Godly Zeal

Read Titus 2:11-14.

Zeal is normally defined as great energy or enthusiasm in pursuit of a cause. It is syn-onymous with words like *passion*, *enthusiasm*, and *fervor*. Zeal always has a cause. Zeal always has passion. Zeal is a feeling, but it's more than a feeling; it's an overwhelming enthusiasm that leads to action.

What we need is not just zeal but godly zeal. Paul helps us see that distinction in two passages from Romans (10:2; 12:11).

In Romans 10, Paul described his deep love for the Jews and longing for them to be saved. He said, "They have a zeal for God, but not according to knowledge" (Romans 10:2). Zeal led Jesus to cleanse the temple. Zeal also led the Jews to crucify Jesus. Not all zeal is godly.

Godly zeal is always rooted in the knowledge of God. Knowledge of God does not water down our zeal—it is the impetus for godly zeal. A zeal that does not accord with knowl-edge is dangerous and destructive.

But godly zeal is not only rooted in knowledge; it is boiling with passion. In Romans 12:11, Paul said, "Do not be slothful in zeal, be fervent in spirit." The opposite of being slothful in zeal is being fervent in spirit. Zeal has strong feelings, emotions, and intensity. Zeal affects your spirit. Zeal consumes your emotions. Zeal takes over. Godly zeal is rooted in knowledge and boiling with passion.

Zeal is also manifested in action. Jesus did not walk into the temple and preach a sermon. Jesus walked into the temple and turned over tables. Zeal is not just a feeling. Zeal is an action. Zeal serves. Zeal moves. Zeal is unable to stand still. Godly zeal is a head full of knowledge, a heart full of passion, and a life full of action. And that is what God has saved you for. Nothing less.

What are the three parts of godly zeal?

Why are all three of those parts essential? What happens when any one of those are missing?

How do you see all three of those parts manifested when Jesus overturned the tables?

What is the problem with having zeal but not zeal for God? Why would that be a negative thing?

Of the three parts of godly zeal, which one do you need to cultivate most?

Ablaze with Glory

Read Revelation 1:12-16.

God does not just want a people; He wants a zealous people. This is what it means to love the Lord your God with all your heart, soul, and strength (Deuteronomy 6:5). His intention has always been that our hearts be filled with passion and affection for Him. Zeal is a primary mark of the people of God. God demands it. He hates anything other than it. And we should not settle for anything less than it.

In Revelation 1, we see a vision of Jesus Christ in blazing splendor. We see Jesus, ablaze with glory. Everything about Him, from His robe to His face, is on fire. When you read this description, you are not only gripped by the picture itself but also by the weight of the picture. This is the weight of glory. The blinding blaze of glory.

Surrounding Jesus, ablaze with glory, are seven lampstands, symbolizing seven churches. And these churches are intended to be the bearers of that blaze. They are, in a sense, the holders of the fire. The church is to be the place in which the blazing glory of God is experienced and displayed. God created the church to be on fire with His glory.

That helps us make sense of God's disgust with the church in Laodicea, which was not ablaze with anything (Revelation 3:14-21). This church was neither cold nor hot but lukewarm; it had no passion, intensity, fervency, or enthusiasm.

So many men are like the church in Laodicea. And the saddest part is not that they are lukewarm but that they don't even notice. The normal Christian experience for most men is one of lukewarm religion instead of white-hot passion. And Jesus hates it!

Why? Because Jesus, who is ablaze with glory, created you to be filled with His glory and make His glory known to the nations. The way He intends to do that is by filling you with boiling zeal for Him. The call of Jesus on your life is nothing less than to be set ablaze with zeal as He is ablaze with glory!

How are godly zeal and following the greatest commandment—to love God with your heart, soul, and strength—connected?

Why is zeal not just another character quality to be cultivated but the primary mark of the people of God? Why does God want a zealous people?

If God's people lack zeal, what does that say about them? What does that communicate to a watching world?

Why was God so disgusted with the church in Laodicea?

Would you say that your heart is more lukewarm or burning with zeal? What do you want it to be? How can you cultivate that?

Repent

Read Revelation 3:15-22.

What is the solution for a lukewarm heart? The same solution for a lukewarm church: "Be zealous and repent" (Revelation 3:19). Repent. Why? It is a sin to be lukewarm. We are called to be zealous and to repent of being lukewarm.

God is so disgusted with a lukewarm heart because being lukewarm takes what is most glorious and makes it appear mundane. Our lukewarm hearts cannot make His glory known. Our lukewarm hearts make it appear as if God is of no real value or worth. And yet, most men live with no passion, affection, desire, or longing for God. Being passion-less about God is a sin.

If there is no zeal in your life, you must repent. Acknowledge your lack of passion for God, see it as a sin, ask Him to forgive you for that sin, and then turn from that sin. Repentance is a conscious act to turn from our sin to God. And you need God's help to do this. The way God cultivates zeal in our lives is through a hatred for the lukewarm and our pleading with Him to forgive and change us. And we must ask God to give us a passion for Him.

If you will see your lack of zeal, acknowledge it to God, and tell Him you want more, He will answer that prayer. God rewards those who seek Him (Hebrews 11:6). He wants you to be zealous.

Do not resist the desire in your heart for zeal. Even if it is just a glimmer of desire, pursue it. Start now. Get on your knees, acknowledge your lack of passion, confess it, turn from it, ask God to change it, and then begin turning toward Him in obedience.

In Revelation 3:17, God reveals the reason the church in Laodicea was lukewarm. How do you see that same attitude in your life or in the church?

What is the connection between our self-sufficiency and a lack of passion?

In Revelation 3:20, God says that He is standing at the door of our hearts knocking. He wants to come in. Why does that give us hope for our lukewarm hearts?

What is the solution for a lukewarm heart?

What would it look like to repent of a lukewarm heart?

Be Zealous!

Read Romans 12:1-13.

We are commanded to "be zealous" (Revelation 3:19). This means zeal is not just something we passively hope for; it is something we aggressively pursue. In the same way that our Christian life is both wholly dependent on the work of God and yet cultivated by the constant effort of our Spirit-infused will, so zeal is a work God must do and a work we must pursue (Romans 12:11).

Although we can cultivate zeal in our lives in many different ways, there are two essentials: the Word and the Spirit. To have zeal, we must have a mind filled with the knowledge of God and a spirit continually being set on fire by His Spirit.

If truth is the foundation of zeal, then the Word is essential to zeal. Your zeal will grow as your knowledge of God grows. What we need first, before anything else, is a fresh and consuming vision of Jesus Christ. We need to see Jesus in His blazing glory for our hearts to be filled with blazing zeal. We need to see Jesus as He is revealed in God's Word.

But zeal is not only a matter of the mind; it is a matter of the spirit. "Do not be slothful in zeal, be fervent in spirit" (Romans 12:11). For your spirit to be filled with the same zeal Jesus manifested in the temple, you must be filled with the same Spirit that filled Jesus. The only hope we have of being zealous for God is the Spirit of God lighting our spirits on fire with His presence.

Jesus said, "If anyone thirsts, let him come to me and drink. Whoever believes in me, as the Scripture has said, 'Out of his heart will flow rivers of living water.' Now this he said about the Spirit" (John 7:37–39). We aren't passively filled with the Spirit, and we aren't passively filled with zeal. The more we go after God, the more God's Spirit puts a fire of zeal in our spirit.

In our pursuit of zeal, we must also aggressively fight the sin that kills our zeal for God. The key is this: You must actively pursue things that fuel the fire of zeal for God and actively kill those things that put the fire out.

Why would God consider it a sin to not be zealous? Why is a lack of zeal damaging to you and others?

What are the two ways we cultivate zeal in our lives?

How could the consistent reading of God's Word impact the amount of zeal you have for God? How does God's Word fight off a lukewarm heart?

If zeal is a work of the Spirit, how can you pursue that? How can you seek more of the Spirit? What does it mean to be filled with the Spirit?

Sin kills zeal. Are there any sins in your life that could be keeping you from the zeal God has for you? What's your battle plan to fight those?

Setting the Temperature

Read Titus 2:5-16.

God's desire is for the heart of every man to be burning with passion for Him. The temperature of a man's heart determines the temperature of a man's home. This is also true of the church. The temperature of our hearts affects everyone around us.

In some supernatural and unexplainable way, God has so ordained it that the men set the temperature. Men can raise the heat or chill the air. And this is not determined by our intentions, hopes, or desires—this is determined by the temperature of our hearts.

The first battle we fight, every day, is the battle for godly zeal. It is the battle to begin each day by fueling the fire through time in God's Word and pursuit of God's Spirit. It continues throughout the day as you aggressively fight any sin or distraction that might diminish the fire. The fire of godly zeal must be your great pursuit.

Think about the perfect zeal of Jesus. Think about Him being overcome with white-hot affection for His Father and His Father's house. Think about the love of God the Father displayed in the sacrifice of His only Son to redeem a people for Himself who would possess the same kind of zeal as His Son. Think about Jesus, captured, beaten, and publicly shamed to bring us to glory. Think about the cost of saving us and making us into a zealous people.

And now think about the disposition of the normal man in church on Sunday mornings. Where is the zeal for God? The men should be singing the loudest, raising their hands the highest, serving the most sacrificially, and listening the most intently.

Men, there is too much at stake in these times for us to settle for anything less than godly zeal. The current of our culture is too strong. The headwinds against the mission are too great. The darkness of the world is too overwhelming. The attacks of the enemy are too strong. We need men filled with godly zeal.

Do you see zeal manifested in the men of your church? If not, why do you think that is?

Have you ever thought about zeal and how much it matters to God? What has the Lord taught you this week about zeal? How has it stirred your heart?

The first battle we fight every day is the battle for zeal. How can you more faithfully and aggressively engage in that battle every day? What does that look like?

How can you challenge the men around you, especially the men in your church, to be more zealous for God?

How can you manifest more zeal, particularly in relationship to your local church?

Week 10

Investments

Group Study

START

Welcome to the final week of **The Titus Ten.**
Use this page to get the conversation going.

To wrap up our time together, we're going to talk about investment. What we're learning is not only for us but also for the men who come after us. We must choose to make an investment.

What have you learned through this study that you're going to put into practice moving forward?

What does it look like to invest in someone?

In his classic book on discipleship, Robert Coleman said: "It all started by Jesus calling a few men to follow him. This revealed immediately the direction his evangelistic strategy would take. His concern was not with programs to teach the multitudes, but with men whom the multitudes would follow. Remarkable as it may seem, Jesus started to gather these men before he ever organized an evangelistic campaign or even preached a sermon in public. Men were to be his method of winning the world to God."[5]

"Men were to be his method." You can spend as much time as you want on the methods of Jesus, but in the end, you will discover His primary method was people. Jesus invested in men who would then lead other men who would go on to lead families, churches, and communities for the glory of God. People are the mission, and people are the method.

WATCH

Use this page to take notes as you watch video session 10.

To access the teaching sessions,
use the instructions in the back
of your Bible study book.

DISCUSS

Use this page to facilitate the group discussion.

The apostle Paul believed in investment. He had not only heard about this method from the disciples, but experienced it from others. Paul's embodied a life of investments made and investments received.

Read Acts 9:26-30. How did Barnabas invest in Paul? Why was Barnabas's investment in Paul so important?

Read 2 Timothy 2:1-2. What was Paul's method of discipleship? How do you see this in Paul's life?

Why are the kinds of investments Paul made in Timothy and Titus so important in the building of God's men?

It was Barnabas, the great encourager, who first vouched for Paul and invested in him when the other disciples were afraid of him (Acts 9:26-30). If it was not for Barnabas, it's hard to believe the disciples would have ever welcomed Paul. From that moment on, a beautiful friendship emerged between Paul and Barnabas. Their gifts and passions were a perfect fit, and together they planted and encouraged many churches. And it all started with Barnabas's decision to make a risky investment.

From that moment on, investing in others was a part of Paul's DNA. We see it clearly in his investment of young Timothy and his call for Timothy to make that same investment in others (2 Timothy 2:1-2). And the book of Titus shows us the way in which Paul invested in Titus.

Who has invested in you in this way?

How could this type of intentional investing in others change your life or the church?

Where do you feel like God is calling you to invest your time and energy for His kingdom?

This is how God builds men: investments. It is how He will build you into a godly man and it is how He will use you to build other men. Godly manhood demands investments.

End your time together by praying for one another. Remind the group to complete the five days of personal study prior to the next group meeting.

Teach & Model

Read Titus 2:1-15.

After identifying godly men, putting them into leadership, and teaching them how to lead the church, Paul told Titus what else he must do: "Teach what accords with sound doctrine" (Titus 2:1).

Paul knew for the church to thrive, every person needed to know how to live. And Paul knew they would get this clarity from both right doctrine and right living, or application of that doctrine. Paul concluded this practical instruction by telling Titus to "declare these things; exhort, and rebuke with all authority. Let no one disregard you" (Titus 2:15). People need the kind of sound doctrine that leads to a solid life.

But Titus was not only to "teach" these things; he was to "model these things." Paul said, "Show yourself in all respects to be a model of good works, and in your teaching show integrity, dignity, and sound speech that cannot be condemned, so that an opponent may be put to shame, having nothing evil to say about us" (Titus 2:7-8).

This word *model* means an example, pattern, or prototype (1 Corinthians 10:6; Philippians 3:17; 1 Thessalonians 1:7). What that church needed was not only a good teacher; they needed a good model. They had never seen a prototype of a godly man. These were first-generation Christians. They needed to hear the truth declared, and they needed to see the truth worked out in real life.

Every man needs to hear sound teaching and see good examples. Every man needs a prototype of godliness. Many passages of Scripture show that this is a role the father is to fulfill for his son (Deuteronomy 6; Psalm 128; 1 Thessalonians 2:11; 1 Timothy 3:2-5). But as strange as it might seem, men need more than that. Even if a man has a godly father, he still needs other men to invest in him. This is why every man needs a church. It is in the ministry of the home and the church that men get hear the teaching and see the models of what it means to be a godly man.

Why is teaching others sound doctrine an important part of becoming the man God wants you to be?

In what ways and from whom are you consistently hearing sound doctrine?

Why are models of godly living important to becoming the man God wants you to be?

Who are models to you of godly manhood? What have you learned from them?

Why is the combination of teaching and modeling so essential? What could be the results in a man's life if one of those were missing?

Generational Investments

Read Psalm 78:1-8.

For the church to fulfill its God-given role of investing in men, it needs both older men and younger men. Because both older men and younger men are critical to spiritual growth, Titus 2 instructs both groups. The instruction to older men is important because these men are called to be a prototype, a model, for the younger men.

To an older man, Paul said, "be sober-minded, dignified, self-controlled, sound in faith, in love, and in steadfastness" (Titus 2:2). This means an older man should avoid extravagances and overindulgences. It means an older man should be distinguished, serious-minded, and have qualities others respect. He should not be frivolous, trivial, or superficial, but his life should be marked by maturity. He should have discernment, discretion, and good judgment that come from walking with God.

He should also be sound in faith, love, and steadfastness. To be sound means to be healthy, proper, and whole. It means to be solid as a rock. And an older man who loves Jesus should be solid as a rock in his faith, love, and steadfastness. An older man should be well-grounded, wise, and unwavering. He should know how to endure hardship, to accept disappointments and failures. He should avoid the temptation and disgrace of trying to act like a younger man. The church needs godly older men. The younger men need godly older men.

There are very few contexts in our culture in which older men and younger men are cultivating relationships. This is a problem. If you only spend time with people your age, you are missing out on the kind of investment God has created you for. Younger men need older men and older men need younger men.

What older men do you know that model Paul's description in Psalm 78 and Titus 2?

What have you learned from these men?

Why do younger men need the investment of older men?

Why it is so important that men find these relationships within the local church?

How can you be involved—personally and through the ministry of your church—in connecting older men and younger men so that they can make an investment in each other?

You Need an Investor

Read Proverbs 18:1.

Almost every start-up company needs investors. An investor is someone who believes in the company and will invest financial capital for the company to grow and expand. A more engaged investor might even invest his business expertise to help the company make good decisions. Companies need investors to succeed. So do you.

We all need people who believe in us, see potential in us, and want to invest in our future. To become the man God wants you to be, you need godly men to invest in you. Sometimes this is through more formal, long-term investment, and sometimes it's an informal, short-term investment. Most likely, you will need some of both.

Most mature godly men will tell you that they are the product of those who have made an investment in them. Some of those investments were intentional and some of them were more informal. But almost every man is the product of those who have made some kind of investment.

Satan's two greatest weapons in the life of every man are passivity and isolation. We have already talked about passivity, but we often neglect the danger of isolation. Proverbs 18:1 says, "Whoever isolates himself seeks his own desire; he breaks out against all sound judgment." Most men tend toward isolation. Even if it's not social isolation, it's spiritual isolation. For this reason, we must heed the warning and wisdom of Solomon and actively seek out men to invest in us. Isolation kills manhood. We need other men in our lives.

Don't wait for a man to invite you into that process. Take the initiative. And don't over-think it or overcomplicate it. You don't need a man to commit to meet with you every week for the next three years. Start by asking a man you respect for breakfast or lunch. Ask questions. Be honest. Seek his wisdom. And in doing so, you will not only honor the other man, you will benefit greatly.

Where would you benefit from having someone invest in you?

Why are these kinds of investments essential to your life? In other words, how will your life suffer if you don't have people making investments in you?

How has your life already benefited from those who have invested in you, formally or informally.

Why do men so often tend toward isolation and resist friendships and mentors? Do you see that temptation in your life?

Who are some men you would like to invest in you? How can you pursue a relationship with them?

You Need to Make an Investment

Read 2 Timothy 2:1-2.

As you spend time with the Lord, grow in your faith, and pursue others to make investments in you, God will invest things in you He intends for you to invest in others. Isn't this the way 2 Timothy 2:2 works? What has been invested in you, you invest in others.

When it comes to making investments in the lives of others, we tend to over-complicate it. And when we over-complicate it, we feel inadequate. You must fight the feeling of inadequacy by reminding yourself of this simple truth: God has invested much in you. Your responsibility is simply to take what God has invested in you and invest it in others.

Part of this investment is biblical truth and spiritual disciplines. When God teaches us new truths from His Word, those need to be invested. When God teaches you how to gain victory over sin and temptation, that is something to invest in others. Any biblical truth or practical application of that truth is something that has been invested in you.

But our investment in others is more than just the investment of biblical truths. Although the primary means by which God teaches us truth is His Word, He also teaches us through others, through experiences, and through suffering. Everything from your background, to your family, to your work, to your greatest highs and your deepest lows, are investments God has made in you. And those are the things God wants you to invest in others.

The great irony of investing in others is that it is always an investment in yourself. Some of the greatest growth in your life will come from the investments you make in the lives of others. The more you resist the temptation to be isolated and choose to invest in others, the more the Lord will invest in you.

What is the model of discipleship from 2 Timothy 2:1-2. From these verses, what does that say about how you should be making investments in others?

Take a moment to write down some specific things the Lord has taught you about how to walk with Him? How could others benefit from that?

Take a moment to write out some specific experiences you have had in your life. How could others benefit from that?

How have you experienced the joy and reward of investing in others?

Who are some people you could begin to invest in? What practical steps can you take to move in that direction?

A Humbling Reminder

Read Judges 2:8-15.

No generation in the Old Testament experienced more of God's supernatural power and blessing than Joshua's generation. This is the generation that finally possessed the promised land and experienced the fullness of all the promises God had made to their ancestors. No generation had more invested in them than Joshua's generation.

But Judges 2:10 says, "And all that generation also were gathered to their fathers. And there arose another generation after them who did not know the LORD or the work that he had done for Israel." The rest of the book of Judges is a humbling reminder of how quickly the next generation can lose all the blessings their fathers experienced. The rest of the Old Testament reveals the consequences.

What happened? How could everything be lost so quickly? The answer seems to be that Joshua's generation, while having so much invested in them and enjoying so much of the fruit of that investment, failed to pass it on to the next generation.

Joshua's generation neglected the clear instructions God gave his people before they entered into the promised land. The Lord told them they not only needed to love Him with all their hearts and guard their hearts from idols, but they must also ensure the next generation heard of the faithfulness of the Lord (Deuteronomy 6). Their failure to invest led to the complete failure of the next generation. This is a humbling reminder of our need to continually invest in others.

This is not just about you. This is about the next generation. This is about God's means by which He intends to use you in the lives of those who come after you. So much has been invested in you. This means you have so much to invest—more than you could ever imagine. Don't let the enemy tell you something different. God wants to use you to make an investment that will long outlive your life.

What might have caused Joshua's generation, which experienced so many great things from the Lord, to fail to invest in the next generation? Where might we be in the same danger?

What does the reading from Judges 2 teach us about the need to invest in others?

How has the previous generation invested in you? What difference has this made in your life?

Who do you feel the Lord wants you to invest in? Start with those closest to you and move outward. Think about your domains.

What keeps you from investing in others? How can you overcome those things and begin making an investment in other men now?

J. Josh Smith

THE TITUS TEN

Bible Study

FOUNDATIONS *for* **GODLY MANHOOD**

Leader Guide

At the beginning of 2008, just two years into my first senior pastor position, I began to feel a need to raise up men in my local church. I was looking for men who were passionate about Jesus, committed to the church, and loved their families. I wanted men of character who knew doctrine and could lead. What I really needed was help! Specifically, I needed the helpt of godly men.

In the fall of that year, I invited ten men to spend ten weeks with me walking through the book of Titus verse by verse. I chose Titus because it had everything I wanted to invest in men. It clarified the need for godly men, the character of godly men, and the consequences of being ungodly men. It helped men understand the centrality of the local church, the need to love their families, and how to be faithful in the workplace. The more I taught from Titus, the more I realized that those forty-six verses really could be a manual for manhood.

After eight years of doing this study almost every semester, I had personally taken 120 men through *The Titus Ten*, ten at a time. It changed that church, and the fruit is still there today. I believe it was the most important thing I did in my eleven-year ministry there.

Over the years, the material changed but the heart stayed the same. Although my heartbeat is verse-by-verse exposition, I felt that this study was better served topically. So, that's what you'll find in *The Titus Ten* Bible study.

This study was, and still is, my first step in developing godly men—but it is not the last. I see this as an entry point into manhood. If I can get a man to be willing to spend ten weeks with me to talk about manhood, and the content resonates with him and begins to change him, then I have a man I can work with.

So, this study is intended to be a first step of sorts. Not an end. After doing this study, think carefully about what is next for your men. Men need to keep moving, and *The Titus Ten* can help them get started.

DIFFERENT WAYS TO LEAD THIS STUDY

This study was never intended to be done alone. Throughout this study we say that the two greatest enemies of manhood are passivity and isolation. This study was intended to combat both of those head on. And doing this study in a group setting helps fight both of those at the same time.

This study will be dramatically more helpful and better in the context of a multi-generational group. This is the heart of Titus 2 and the heart behind *The Titus Ten* Bible study. This was intended to help foster multi-generational relationships. When those relationships are not found at home, they must be found in the context of the church.

DISCIPLESHIP GROUP: three to five men you are already in community with. If you are already in a discipleship group, home group, or Sunday School group, choose a few men who will commit to meet with you for ten weeks to do this study.

SMALL GROUP STUDY: six to ten men whom you would identify as potential and handpick to do this study with you. This study was originally created to be done with ten men at a time. But it will be easier for men to hide in a group this size, which defeats the purpose. If you do it this way, it would be good to ask one man every week to share his story. If you have ten men and ten weeks, ask every man to choose a week that he will tell his story, then spend the last twenty minutes of the time hearing from him and praying for him.

LARGE GROUP STUDY: This study can work great in a large group setting, from eleven men to hundreds of me, *if* the large group setting is at round tables with table leaders. This study can't just be taught; it must be discussed. Again, the goal is to fight passivity and isolation. If you lead a large group study, the leader can teach the content and then have table leaders lead the discussion time. This is a great way to get a lot of men through the content without allowing them to hide.

If you chose to do it this way, appoint your table leaders ahead of time and invite them to fill their tables, as much as they can, with six or seven men they know. This allows a man to invest in other men without having to lead the entire study. The table leader must ensure his men are there each week, lead the discussion at the end of the teaching, and follow up with and invest in the men throughout the study.

TIPS FOR LEADERS

1. Be personal. The difference between *The Titus Ten* book and *The Titus Ten* Bible study is primarily the illustrations. The illustrations are key to getting these concepts, but when teaching it yourself in a Bible Study format, it is best for the leader to come up with personal illustrations.

As you read over the study and prepare to teach, think carefully about ways you have seen these concepts in your life. Be personal. The more personal and vulnerable you are, the more open others will be. The vulnerability and honesty of the leader will determine the effect of the group as much as anything.

2. Constantly fight isolation and passivity. Do not let men hide in a group or get away with not putting some of these things in practice. Make sure everyone answers questions each week. Make sure everyone has the opportunity to reflect on the previous week. Keep using this study as an opportunity to fight those two great enemies of manhood.

3. Ask the men for more. Men in the church are a generally unchallenged group. Take the opportunity to challenge them. Don't make this too easy. Consider asking them to do things in addition to the study to challenge them. For instance, have the group early in the morning, ask them to read the forty-six verses of Titus a few times a week during the whole study, or ask them to pray with their wives every week during the study. Add something to this process that challenges and moves men.

4. Spend time together outside the group. This content stirs up things in a mans heart. It forces him to think about things he has never thought about. Most men will not be able to process all that in a group setting. Because of that, it is very helpful to commit to some one-on-one time with each of the men outside of the group setting. If you take then men through this, have coffee with one man a week for ten weeks. If you are leading a table of six, meet with every man individually sometime during the ten-week study.

5. Make this a starting place. Think about ministering to men in concentric circles. The largest outer circle can represent corporate worship and the smallest inner circle represents personal intimacy with God. You are trying to move men from the outer circle (just being in the crowd) to the inner circle (intimacy with God). *The Titus Ten* Bible study is a step in that process, but not the end of the process. Make sure they know this. Communicate to men your desire to see them keep moving and then have a pathway that fits your context.

The Titus Ten

Sources

1. Warren Baker and Gene Carpenter, eds., *The Complete Word Study Dictionary* (Chattanooga, TN: AMG Publishers, 2003).

2. *The Collected Works of John Stuart Mill, Volume XXI - Essays on Equality, Law, and Education*, ed. John M. Robson, Introduction by Stefan Collini (Toronto: University of Toronto Press, London: Routledge and Kegan Paul, 1984), accessed October 25, 2023, https://oll.libertyfund.org/title/mill-the-collected-works-of-john-stuart-mill-volume-xxi-essays-on-equality-law-and-education?html=true.

3. David Platt, "Great Commission Statistics That Should Concern US," Radical, May 5, 2021, https://radical.net/article/great-commission-statistics-concern/.

4. Reaching 3000 Unengaged Unreached People Groups," IMB, accessed October 31, 2023, https://www.imb.org/give/project/reaching-3000-uupgs/; "UUPGs: Unengaged Unreached People Groups," Imb.maps.arcgis.com, accessed October 31, 2023, https://imb.maps.arcgis.com/apps/Viewer/index.html?appid=807928071960422291fd231a2dda7e4e.

5. Robert Coleman, *The Master Plan of Evangelism* (Grand Rapids, MI: Revell, 1993), 21.

ALSO AVAILABLE
from
J. Josh Smith

The Titus Ten is a manual for becoming
the kind of man God intends for you to be, and helps
equip you to lead other men to do the same.

Available where books are sold

How to be a Christian man.

Everything in a man's life hinges on the kind of man he is. Yet, none of us is naturally a godly man. That's something we have to learn, pursue, and cultivate.

ADDITIONAL RESOURCES

Bible Study eBook with Video Access
Includes the content of this printed book but offers the convenience and flexibility that comes with mobile technology.

005847303 **$19.99**

DVD Set

005847318 **$29.99**

Price and availability subject to change without notice.

This study can serve as a manual for those seeking to become more godly and to lead other men to do the same.

- Build your character in a way that honors God and those around you.
- Commit to serving God and those entrusted to your care with zeal.
- Start a discipleship movement among men in your church.

Studying on your own?

To enrich your study experience, be sure to access the videos available through a redemption code printed in this *Bible Study Book.*

Leading a group?

Each group member will need *The Titus Ten Bible Study Book,* which includes video access. Because all participants will have access to the video content, you can choose to watch the videos outside of your group meeting if desired. Or, if you're watching together and someone misses a group meeting, they'll have the flexibility to catch up.